Pilgrimage

A Modern Seeker's Guide

PILGRIMAGE

A Modern Seeker's Guide

by Evans Bowen

LABYRINTHINE PRESS

An imprint of AUDREYPRESS

PILGRIMAGE: A MODERN SEEKER'S GUIDE

Editors: Mallory Leonard Adamson
Text Design: Roscoe Welply
Cover Design: Roscoe Welply
First Edition: 2018

Library of Congress Cataloging-in Publication Data has been applied for.

ISBN 978-1-936426-40-9

E-book ISBN: 978-1-936426-41-6

18 19 20 21 22 LSC/C 10 9 8 7 6 5 4 3 2 1

Labyrinthine Press
P.O. Box 6113
Maryville, Tennessee 37802

Contents

Dedication

To my father, **Millard**.

"*An early-morning walk is a blessing for the whole day.*"

Thoreau

Introduction

NEVER BEFORE IN THE HISTORY of mankind has it been so easy for humans to travel. Before the 20th century and train travel, the only means of transportation was by boat, horse or on foot. That made even a trip to the next town a big event. It has really been only in the last few decades that journeying to a distant land stopped being arduous, life-threatening, and out of reach of the ordinary human being. Before then, travel was for intrepid explorers, the very wealthy, or immigrants. I've seen movies and read about explorers who, just a hundred years ago, mapped the uncharted regions of our globe. These endeavors took years, and many didn't return home.

Now, nearly every square mile of the planet has been photographed, and anyone can see anywhere at any time as long as they have access to Google Earth. It is hard to wrap your mind around how quickly our world has changed and how fortunate we are to live in a time when the world as a whole is available to us. It wasn't long ago that our grandparents and great-grandparents left their homelands for new lives in other parts of the world, knowing that returning, even for a visit, was out of the question. As recently as the 1960s, reaching Europe from the United States meant an expensive, week-long journey across the Atlantic on a ship. Air travel—and its commercialization—has changed everything. Until now, the vast majority of people never had the resources or the time to explore beyond their known world.

However, there has always been one group of people who have ventured far from home in pursuit of spiritual growth—pilgrims. For centuries, the faithful have been called to places such as Jerusalem, Santiago, Canterbury, Mecca, and the river Ganges. Prepared for no ordinary pleasure trip, large groups set out on foot, knowing their journey would take months or even years to visit the places that promised healing, salvation, glory, and devotion. Pilgrimages were once-in-a-lifetime trips that required great sacrifice with no guarantee that the pilgrim would even reach the holy shrine or return home.

It is in this spirit of the pilgrims of history that we now bring pilgrimage into modern times for modern seekers. Our world has expanded, and our means of transportation has grown, but the deep longing in our hearts has remained remained as strong as it did for the pilgrims of the past. It is the call of our soul for more meaning, to understand our planet and its people and to find the deepest point in our hearts where the divine spark resides.

It is time to remember what our ancestors knew about sacred sites and holy places, to feel the deep longing of our hearts to touch the Divine and bring meaning to our very material world. This isn't about condemning the material world but using it to work for the modern seeker with access to the world and not letting materialism control the heart and mind. It is time to update the ancient human need for pilgrimage for our modern, fast-paced world. This desire to search for the sacred is still relevant and useful for our modern lives. In fact, it might be needed now more than ever. We may not be walking for salvation bestowed by a church, but we are seeking salvation none-the-less. Life is hard, and if we don't take the time to hear our own voices and reach out for more meaning, we will be swept up in the world and in danger of losing our lives to society, obligations, and fear.

A pilgrimage has two layers, the external and the internal. A physical journey to a place previously unknown to us is symbolic of the inner journey into the unknown parts of our hearts, the seat of our souls' desires. In the outward journey, we challenge our physical bodies to do more, to experience more, and to take risks. The same is true for our hearts. By seeing more in the world, we challenge our hearts to grow. We free ourselves from our social conditioning and gain a new perspective on the world and our lives. A pilgrimage is a process of bringing mind, body, and spirit together for one purpose—to transform the whole person. The Buddha said, "You can't travel the path until you have become the path itself". A pilgrimage creates a sacred space where your physical body and heart can meet and meld into one. As the sacred space opens more light shines in and new vistas, ideas, langages, and experiences bring you to a new place in your life you could never imagine before.

As you take your pilgrimage, you will learn a new language. I don't mean the language of another country; instead, you will build a new vocabulary that allows new thoughts and ideas to become part of your life. I liken it to creating new file folders in your mind. As you learn new things, have new experiences, you add material to these file folders. Now you have a place, a context for new information. This further information is no longer just theory but experience that you can now use and add to throughout your life. Your pilgrimage will inform the rest of your life, opening doors that you previously didn't know existed. Have you ever had the experience of learning a word or about a book or place, then suddenly you notice it everywhere? It was everywhere before you learned it, but you couldn't see it until you had a context for the new idea. The intent and act of pilgrimage teach you a new language that allows you to open your life to these new worlds internally and externally.

In this book, I have used a specific language. It is the language of pilgrimage that I learned from others but most of all from my own experience. I have also purposefully used words that I intend to be spiritually inclusive, such as Universe, Divine, Holy, Sacred. I believe the wisdom of pilgrimage crosses all religions and faiths, speaking to the heart of all human experience. As you go through this book, I invite you to add your own experience, tradition, or non-tradition, and read this book regarding your own spiritual path. My goal is to emphasize the universal nature of the soul's longing for the deepest meaning of life and shared the wisdom of pilgrimage that I have learned over the years. Some of my pilgrimages were short, lasting a few hours or a day. Some were long, taking weeks. My longest pilgrimage, when I walked the Camino de

Santiago with my daughter, lasted five weeks. Each experience was perfect for my life at the time, and I know there are many more pilgrimages in my future. After all, there is always more to discover about life, the world and ourselves.

I invite you to use this book as a guide for your own pilgrimage, however long or short the physical journey may be. No two pilgrimages will ever be the same, just as no two pilgrims ever could be. Whether you travel across an ocean or across town, the lessons of pilgrimage are just as profound. You don't have to go halfway across the world to have a spiritual experience, unless, of course, that's exactly what your soul is longing for. Each of us is called to different places, to different journeys, as we seek our most meaningful and authentic lives. Knowing this, you can trust that your experience will be perfect for you at this time in your life, just as mine have always been for me.

A History of Pilgrimage

PILGRIMAGES SEEM TO BE INNATE, part of the foundation of human nature because all spiritual traditions have some form of a journey to holy places or times to go out into the world to discover the deeper parts of oneself. Throughout the holy books around the world are stories of men leaving the confines and comfort of their community to discover and prove themselves. There are stories of people entering the wilderness to hear the voice of the Divine, or find the inner strength to prove one's worth or prepare for an important mission or destiny. Now we have the opportunity to make pilgrimage universal for men, women, old, young, religious, not religious— to answer the call of the human spirit.

Over the last few millennia, pilgrimages have taken many forms and proven to be an invaluable tool in the quest for meaning and purpose. Let us look at the religious traditions from around the world and see how they have used pilgrimage. From these examples, you can see what a significant experience a quest for the Divine is for the development of our souls.

The Christian story begins with a pilgrimage. The three wise men travel to see the new baby Jesus and bring him offerings. Throughout the Bible, there are stories of going to the desert, wilderness, or mountains to seek answers and find strength. Many of these stories connect to the number 40, and in the second half of the book, we will use this number as a guide for your pilgrimage. In the Bible, the number 40 is used to indicate a time for a trial or initiation that results in transformation. For example, the flood was 40 days and nights. The Israelites wandered in the desert for 40 years. Jesus was in the wilderness for 40 days and nights being tempted by the Devil.

Christians have continued this tradition starting with visits to the Desert Fathers in the 300s to seek wisdom. Jerusalem, as well as Canterbury, England, and Santiago, Spain became the three most important pilgrimages of medieval Europe. Millions of pilgrims walked from their front doors hundreds even thousands of miles to these holy places. The world was changed by these pilgrims interacting then returning home with new experiences and sharing the information they'd learned from other cultures.

After the Reformation, pilgrimage fell out of favor when salvation was no longer linked to indulgences—methods of reducing the punishment for sin, such as repeating a prayer, performing good works or visiting a specific holy place. At this time Christian pilgrimage was replaced by walking the Stations of the Cross inside the local church. The Camino de Santiago has only come back into popularity in the last few decades. The same is true for the pilgrimage to Canterbury to the shrine of Thomas Beckett. Students still read about this famous journey in Chaucer's Canterbury Tales, but otherwise, the journey was long abandoned.

Over the last century the places of Mary sightings, such as Lourdes and Fatima, have drawn many believers from around the world in search of healing and blessings. As these new sites have gained popularity, they have also gained the power to heal and give hope to the pilgrims who come with deep devotion. The pilgrimage sites have grown to accommodate the physical and spiritual needs of the pilgrim and reflect the evolving nature of pilgrimages.

Pilgrimage is an integral part of the Islamic religion and is one of the five pillars of Islam and dates back to the time of Abraham. Every year millions of Muslims visit Mecca in Saudi Arabia as part of the Hajj. This annual gathering is the largest in the world and is required once in the lifetime of all adult Muslims who are financially and physically able. The word Hajj means "to intend a journey" and refers to the physical trip as well as to spiritual intentions, the true meaning of pilgrimage. The exterior journey reflects an interior act of intention. During the Hajj the devotees perform specific rituals including the most well-known, walking around the Ka'aba seven times.

Jews have three pilgrimage festivals every year which reaffirm their commitment to God. These three festivals were initially part of the requirements to travel to Jerusalem. The Western Wall on the Temple Mount in Jerusalem is the holiest site in the Jewish tradition and to this day calls thousands every year for prayer.

Buddhism has a tradition of pilgrimage to sites that are significant to the Buddha's life story, and there are many shrines that draw pilgrims to pay homage to the Buddha and his path of enlightenment. Hindus are not required to take a pilgrimage but many sacred sites throughout India, Pakistan, and Nepal draw pilgrims to worship, and there are many rituals performed at the sacred river Ganges. In Japan, there are many shrines, and there is a tradition of visiting the 88 temples on the island of Shikoku as well as the sacred Mt. Fuji.

The Greeks and Romans saw pilgrimage as the hero's journey, as in the story of Ulysses. In *The Odyssey*, Ulysses sets out on an adventure, faces crisis and temptations, triumphs and comes home transformed. He brings knowledge and experience back to his home and people to help transform them too. These tales of heroism are still retold today and are the inspiration for books and movies such as *Star Wars* and *Lord of the Rings*.

In all of these traditions are the two threads running through all pilgrimages: initiation, and devotion. The pilgrim has a call of devotion to a holy place to honor a deity, ideal or experience. During this pilgrimage, an initiation into higher understanding, expanded experience or intense trial brings new devotion to life, the community and the sacred.

As world travel has become more accessible to the average person, ancient sites have called a new group of pilgrims seeking the ancient wisdom of such iconic sites as Stonehenge, Machu Picchu, and the Great Pyramids. Many of these places such as Petra, Jordan, have only been rediscovered in the modern era. Their rediscovery is an indication of the reawakening of new wisdom in our world. As we have learned more about our remarkable earth new sacred sites, such as Sedona, Arizona, are rising to reflect our understanding and respect for the earth's energy system. Our planet is alive and changing as we humans also change. We now have the technology and access to discover and rediscover our world from invisible particles to the depths of distant galaxies, reflecting whole new undiscovered worlds within ourselves. As our lifetimes lengthens we have more time to find new pathways for human consciousness to expand. We must each find the curiosity that leads us down our individual paths of discovery and re-enchantment for our lives and the world around us.

As our world changes with air travel and the internet, our idea of pilgrimage naturally has to change as well. We now take pilgrimages to bring about inner change, to give a meaningful experience to our spirituality, to mark a critical turning point in our life or to fulfill a lifelong dream. But just because the pilgrimage is a choice rather than a religious command, it is no less meaningful. Actually, it becomes even more personal, a quest to be initiated into a greater awareness of ourselves, our lives and our place in the cosmos. It is a time to take the beauty and devotion and inner longing of the great tradition of pilgrimage and make it your own—your own quest, your own time, your own healing and your own sacred tradition. No two pilgrims are alike, and no two pilgrimages will ever be the same. Our modern world allows us to make a pilgrimage meaningful to our lives and unique circumstances. Pilgrimage is about devotion and initiation and transformation. It is a journey from one way of seeing to another. The specifics are between you and the Divine.

Part 1

Stages of Pilgrimages

The Call

IT COMES AS A WHISPER, an overheard conversation, a mention in the paper, a longing from childhood, a desire. The Call is the first stage in the transformational process we call pilgrimage. The Call is a catalyst to seek out more of life, to take your life to a new level. The Call comes when you are ready. You might not think you are ready, but your soul and spirit are wanting more. This summons from the depth of your heart and soul is the first step on your journey.

I heard the first whispers of my call when I read Shirley MacLaine's book *The Camino: A Journey of the Spirit*. In this book, MacLaine walks 500 miles on the thousand-year-old Spanish pilgrimage route from the Pyrenees mountains to the holy city of Santiago. At the time, I didn't even recognize that I was being called. I had young children at the time, and a pilgrimage was not in the realm of the possible. A few years ago the Camino started to show up more often in my life. First I read a book, for fun, called "*What the Psychic Told the Pilgrim: A Midlife on Spain's Camino de Santiago*" by Jane Christmas. The author had walked the Camino to mark an important birthday and the end of her marriage. That led me to read several other books, including a catalog on flower essences that highlighted the significance of Camino flowers. Eventually, the references came more quickly and obviously. I made a friend with a house in Spain and who also felt a longing to go. The Camino was brought into popular culture by the film *The Way*. Finally, I read yet another book about a young woman, a dancer, who walked the Camino to transition into adulthood. When I passed this book on to my daughter Alexandra, I started to realize that I was being called to the Camino myself.

Alexandra was about 20 at the time and became as enchanted with the idea as I was. "Mom, we must do this," she insisted constantly. "We have to walk the Camino the summer before my senior year of college." Partly because I couldn't say no to an adventure with my girl before she left home, and partly because I knew I needed precisely this challenge for my own life, I answered the call.

So we started to make our plans. We chose to leave right after school finished in May, which also happened to be just days after my 50th birthday. Just as this time marked a huge transition for my daughter, I was struggling with my own in-between. My children were all grown up, and I had just finished five intense years of caring for my in-laws at the end of their lives. I really wasn't sure what to do next. The walk came as a perfect goal to send me into the second half of my life with a physical, mental and spiritual adventure.

SACRED SITES

The Camino has become a very well known pilgrimage, but it is just one of many famous pilgrimage sites around the world. Many pilgrims are called to places of spiritual power such as the Great Pyramids, Stonehenge, Lourdes, Mecca and great cathedrals. People come from all over the world to be in the energy of these sites and absorb their wisdom. These great places of spirit hold the devotion and prayers of all the pilgrims who have come before. These places are "thin" spots where the Divine shines through more easily, and that's why we feel called to them.

Any place of worship can be a sacred site: temples, mosques, cathedrals, churches, places built by humans for prayer and religious learning. The well-known sites like Chartres Cathedral are easy to identify, and when you're there, you can't miss the power of these places. But sacred sites don't necessarily have to draw huge crowds. Anywhere there has been prayer has been made holy.

Sites may also be made sacred by the weight of their histories, such as Petra in Jordan or the Parthenon in Greece. These sites hold the story of humanity. We go there to honor the great achievements of our ancestors, the memory of where we come from and the wisdom of the great thinkers and builders of the past.

The sites that hold our memories of sorrow can be powerful places: battlefields, graves, war memorials, Holocaust museums. It is easy to want to remember only happy times, but our lives are also made up of hard and painful times of grief. A pilgrimage to these sites is a time for catharsis. We need a place to put the grief we can no longer carry for our selves and the grief of our collective humanity.

Sometimes what we need most in our lives is solitude and quiet so we can have time to listen to our heart. Taking pilgrimages to monasteries, ashrams, retreat centers or places of quiet feed the soul. Silence is soothing and allows you to rest. Silence is the language of the Divine.

There are places where holy events took place, like the apparitions of Mother Mary at Lourdes and Fatima, Assisi, Italy where Saint Francis lived, Delphi, Greece, where the oracle made great prophesies, and Bethlehem where Christ was born. These places are infused with the magic of undeniable divine presence. Many places associated with holy events then become sites of healing both physical and spiritual because the energy and hope the place holds, makes such miracles possible.

Sacred stones call us as well, including sites like Stonehenge in England, Carnac in France and Callanish in Scotland. Rocks hold memory and energy. They were used by the ancients as energy markers, like acupuncture points on the land. There is still great mystery around these sacred stones, and the call of these places is undeniable.

Wells, rivers, lakes, and oceans all have the call of the sacred. Holy rivers like the Ganges and the Jordan have special meaning. Sacred wells such as the Chalice Well in Glastonbury, England have been used for healing and anointing for hundreds of years. Lourdes has a spring and baths for healing miracles. But it's not just the 'blessed' waters that call to pilgrims. A pilgrimage to any body of water that speaks to your soul can be healing, nourishing, rejuvenating.

The natural beauty of our world gives us the wonder and awe of the divine. The Grand Canyon, the Redwood forests, Yellowstone, the Galapagos Islands all hold the magnificence of our planet. These living cathedrals need nothing more to be holy. These places inspire and humble us at the same time. To be in the presence of beauty is to be in the presence of God. Earth is a sacred being, and sacred sites are our classrooms. We are all so so lucky to live on this beautiful planet, and pilgrimage is one way we can show our gratitude.

Many ancient sacred sites are copies of the heavens. The ancients knew the power of the stars, sun, and moon. Sites like Stonehenge and Machu Picchu in Peru are astronomical sites that aligned with solstices and equinoxes. The Camino in Spain is aligned to the path of the Milky Way. The Pyramids are aligned to the constellation Orion, making them a map of heaven on earth. The sites remind us that we are part of an infinite, mysterious universe and help us tap into the awe and wonder of the stars and galaxies.

A sacred site has a presence that you can feel. This is where the holy shines through the mundane. Prayers, beauty, miracles, sacred arrangement, and alignment with the heavens create an energy, an imprint on the land and on those who come to it with devotion. Pilgrims not only receive blessings from these sites but also give back their energy and love. This interaction feeds the site and links the stream of devotion to the timeless Divine. There is a conscious interaction between the pilgrim and the land. The pilgrim is forever part of the land, and the land is forever part of the pilgrim.

You get to discover and decide which places are sacred in

your life. You may feel called to a site such as the Pyramids or a magnificent cathedral, but you can just as quickly find what you are looking for in your own backyard. The main component of any place that you find sacred is the awe, wonder, peace, and healing that you experience there. These are the places that help you remember your true identity as a beloved child of the Divine.

Is there a sacred place that calls to you? If so, it is time to answer the call, to journey to the place that your soul longs for—your sacred site.

The Call to a pilgrimage comes in many forms and for many reasons. It can be a longing to see the world differently, to connect with yourself and the world more deeply, to look for inner peace or to heal a broken heart. It is time to do something different, to shake up your world, so you don't let life pass you by. This is a time for rejuvenation, healing, catharsis, devotion. This mindful/soulful travel isn't about entertainment but seeking deep meaning, deep healing of life. This isn't about a schedule or ticking off a list. Pilgrimage is about being humble and open to the experience that calls your soul to expand. You are asking to become changed.

When the Call comes, you can't ignore it. It may come in many ways; a dream, a shock, an illness or loss. Sometimes the call comes in a moment of darkness when you just can't go on. Then comes a knock on the door of your heart. It is a turning point in your life; it is your soul coming to bring the needed changes, to open you to new possibilities. This is the pull of your higher self— asking to be recognized and nurtured to be your full and authentic self. The Call means you need to take time to hear your own inner voice and your own heart, away from the world you know, and to give your heart and mind and body a physical challenge to prove that you can be so much more.

When you accept the Call to go, the unseen forces of your life rise to meet you, to move you toward your soul's longing. It might not be a 500-mile walk but it could be to an exotic land that holds information, energy, an experience that you feel missing from your life. It could be a cross-country drive. It can be a stroll around the corner to remember a part of your life you had buried or forgotten. The Call will come to move your life in the direction that you long for, that your soul needs to fulfill your purpose.

A pilgrimage helps you find that secret space where you step out of your ordinary life and take time to listen to the longing of your heart and to find your extraordinary life. So take time to hear your Call. Take time in silence, hear the quiet voice of your heart and know that is your soul calling you to the next stage of your journey through life.

Preparation

YOU HAVE HEARD THE CALL, and you have chosen your destination. Now is the time to move to the second phase of your pilgrimage, your journey deeper into your soul and spirit. You are already on your journey, have already started the changes. When you decided to act, to answer the call of the heart, you set in motion the energy needed to fulfill your heart's desire.

When I answered the call to the Camino, I began the preparation. There was a lot to be done to make my trip successful. I had one big goal, and that was to finish the entire trip and make the whole experience as joyful as possible. That meant I needed to make sure I had all the right equipment, I was physically ready to walk 500 miles, and I was able to leave home and not worry. I wanted to be free to concentrate on my experience. First I read several books on the practical side of the walk. I visited my local backpacking store because I had never backpacked. I needed an expert to make sure I had what worked best for me. I enjoyed the research and spent many hours thinking and reading about the practicalities. All of this paid off because the thinking part was done and I could then move to the experience part.

Alexandra and I had so much fun choosing our equipment and preparing for our trip. My mother gifted us sleeping bags for Christmas. We used Spring Break time to load the packs and walk around the neighborhood to get our legs use to a long walk. I laid out everything, checking and rechecking to make sure that we had everything we needed. Every moment of planning and anticipation was fun and a part of the journey.

Anticipation is part of our lives. In Christianity, there are two times in the church calendar devoted to anticipation: Lent and Advent. Lent is the time of prayer and sacrifice leading to Easter. Advent is the time to prepare for Christmas. These are the times of the year that expectation is honored, understood to be part of our lives. The talking and planning for a future event are as important as the event itself. Enjoy this time of learning and preparing. Enjoy the anticipation. This is just as important a part of the process of transformation as the actual journey for all the parts of the process are, in fact, the journey.

This is a phase of both dream and practicality. No pilgrimage will succeed without some planning. After you have decided where you want to go, what special place on earth has called you, then you have to choose a date. How much time do you have for travel? What time of year is best for your journey regarding weather, crowds, holidays? For some pilgrimages, this phase is rather short. Some journeys need months to prepare.

Who do you want to travel with? Do you want to go by yourself, with a companion or two, family or friends or a tour group and guide? What works best for your pilgrimage? This very much depends on your destination. Some places require a group or guide, sometimes for safety, sometimes for convenience. I traveled in a group to Egypt and Peru, neither place I would have been comfortable on my own. With the details taken care of by the guide, I could relax and just enjoy every place without worry about transportation or accommodations. I've traveled to England and Scotland with family, and we made all our own arrangements. I've traveled alone in France and the United States and done everything literally by myself. What works best for your pilgrimage?

What travel arrangements do you need? You need to have your tickets, itinerary, passport and possibly a visa. All of this needs to be taken care of in advance. I highly recommend travel insurance in case of illness or injury; basic coverage can be inexpensive and goes a long way for peace of mind. You need to learn the customs of your destination and at least some basic words in the local language. Interacting with the local people is such an enjoyable part of your adventure and one of the richest parts of the experience.

What do you physically need to take? What equipment and clothing are required for your destination? Research the weather and terrain, so you know the best clothing and shoes to bring. Break in your travel shoes so you won't get blisters that can really take the fun out of your adventure. Which is better for your trip, a suitcase or backpack? I had to do a lot of research for my Camino pilgrimage since I had never backpacked. All the time and attention I paid to details made me well prepared and the trip more enjoyable. The most important thing about traveling as a pilgrim is to pack lightly. This isn't about being fashionable but practical and simple. A pilgrim packs only what they need. Don't burden yourself with possessions to lose. The more you take, the more you have to look after.

What do you have to do to leave your home? Do you need someone to help with your children or pets? Do you need to get extra work done before you leave? It always seems to take a week for me to prepare the house and office to leave. I need to make sure bills are paid that come due while I'm gone. I need my house to be clean and taken care of. I need to stock the refrigerator or empty it depending on who is staying at home.

You need to prepare your physical body for your trip. If you don't have a regular exercise routine now is the time to start walking more regularly. Travel usually means extensive walking and stairs so the more fit you are, the more comfortable you will be. Gather any medications you will need and special medications specific to your trip. If you have food restrictions, have some food with you and print out instructions in the language of your destination. Physical preparation is as important as the spiritual, as the body strengthens so does the mind and heart.

It is also time to prepare your mind. Research the history, customs, architecture, art, music of your destination. The more familiar you are with your pilgrimage, the more easily you can enjoy the experience. Just like knowing a song before you hear it in a concert, the more you know a place, the easier and more enjoyable your travel will be. This is also the time to manage your apprehensions, both real and imagined before facing the unknown and unfamiliar. How will you record your journey? With journaling, photos, souvenirs? This journey is a blank book or canvas ready to unfold before you. A word of caution about photos, please don't experience your trip behind the camera so that you live it only in the future through your pictures. Take a few photos to remember but then put down the camera and just experience the subtleties of the place. Recording should only take a few minutes, the rest of the time needs to be about your personal interaction with this sacred place.

Prepare your heart for your journey. A pilgrim is humble and open to what this sacred journey will bring. This is the time to understand your motive for taking this journey. Make sure you have the right motives and expectations. This is a time for an open mind and heart to be able to accept the experiences and changes that are part of being a pilgrim. You are asking for change and growth, and that is never easy. You may want to do some spiritual or religious rituals before your journey. You might also seek the blessing of a religious leader, a special dedication to your quest or a purification ritual.

Bring something into your environment that reminds you daily of your adventure. I like to add the weather for my upcoming destination on my weather app so that I get familiar with the climate and it is another way to anticipate my journey. You might also want to gather gifts for your local contacts and the children at your destination. I always took ink pens for the children in Egypt. One friend brought a suitcase full of stuffed animals to give away to the local children.

It is also traditional to bring gifts or offerings to the sacred site. This is where you need to use discretion since you don't want to do anything that is illegal or would harm the site. I have left a traditional token, such as tobacco or cornmeal, or a small flower or tiny stone as an offering, These don't disturb the site's environment but show your sincere appreciation for its blessing. Remember your love and prayers are the greatest gifts you can give and sometimes these are all you need to give to receive the blessing of the sacred site.

You have made your plans, but serendipity and synchronicity will play a part in the journey for it is in the unexpected that spirit and the universe will present their gifts. These are the moments of surprise and wonder that make the journey life-changing. This is the time to find your flexibility, willingness, strength, and courage. Your awareness is heightened, and your intuition is open to the possibilities. The more you are prepared for the quest, the freer your mind can be to take in the newness. You can leave your worries knowing you have prepared everything you need and now it is time to take the next step. Take time now to relax and refocus before you walk out your front door.

Leaving

THE DAY YOU HAVE ANTICIPATED for so long has finally arrived. The next stage of the journey is here: the time to close the door behind you and move into the unknown of the pilgrimage. This can be exciting and a bit scary too. Managing your fears as well as excitement is part of being a pilgrim. Fears and anxiety show up when we push on the edges of our known world. But don't let this discourage you, this is a time for courage and courage is an integral part of the pilgrim's heart.

It took courage for me to set off on a five-week walk in a foreign country. I was leaving my life for an intensely new and unknown journey. I had a guidebook, and I had prepared but there were plenty of things I couldn't anticipate and that made me anxious, and I was also responsible for the health and safety of my daughter. But, at the same time, I was excited for the adventure too. Don't be worried about the mixed emotions of your journey; it is part of the process.

In the hustle of last-minute details try to slow down and make this important transition. Every part of the journey is important and the moment of leaving has its own unique qualities. This is a liminal time, an in-between time. You are leaving the comfortable for the challenging. You are crossing the threshold. This is the moment that you move into life as a pilgrim.

I encourage you to make a ritual of this time. As I leave for a pilgrimage, I take a ritual bath, consciously consecrating my body for the journey. I choose this ritual because I want to cleanse my mind as well as my body before embarking on a new path. Water symbolizes rebirth and blessing, and that is exactly what I experience at this stage of pilgrimage. You are transforming from mundane life to a spiritual path. By ritualizing the departure, you mark a specific time, set a specific space and energy. From now on everything has meaning. You are starting to live your ideal, to move out and quest. You have only an idea of where you are going or who you will become. A pilgrimage is not an escape from life but a purposeful step into the unknown of the world and yourself.

You say goodbye to your friends and family; they are there to wish you well on your journey. They have anxiety, too, about what you will face. When I left for the Camino, I spent several days saying goodbye. Every day for I met with friends to talk about the adventure and share with them my excitement. These were special moments to share and get their blessing.

When I leave for a big adventure, I try to make sure that I'm not rushed, that I have everything ready so that I'm not worried I'm forgetting something. I put on the clothes that I have laid out the day before. My bag is packed, and I do the last few things before walking through the door. Make sure there is time to sit for a minute and meditate or say a prayer, asking for guidance. This is part of preparing the mind, heart, and body to come together as our quest is both physical and spiritual. Every part of the quest needs moments of dedication, an acknowledgment of the process you have undertaken.

You walk through the open door, and it closes behind you. You lock the door, and you are officially a pilgrim. There is a saying that the Camino begins at your front door. This is a single auspicious moment. This is the moment of separation between the everyday world and the sacred journey. A moment when you move from the profane to the sacred. A moment that changes everything. This begins your physical journey, by car, plane, train, foot. It will be awhile before you are back in the comforts of your own home. You are leaving your security, your old self, your known world. It is time to start your transition, time to start your quest for inner gold. You don't know where this journey will go or who you will become, you just know you must go, you must find out.

Journey

THE DOOR CLOSES, and you are officially a pilgrim. It doesn't matter what your transportation. It is all part of the adventure. All methods of transportation have their places. The pilgrim uses whatever means are necessary. You may float down the Nile on a boat, watching the world as it was thousands of years ago. You may be in a car on the 'wrong side' of the road. Maybe you're on a bus in Peru, holding on for dear life as you wind up the steep mountain road, all too aware of the precipitous drop. You might be in for a long, uncomfortable plane ride where multiple movies barely made a dent in the time. Or maybe you take a train across the countryside with the gently swaying lulling you to sleep. You could even be riding a horse up a mountain, praying away fear with every hoof fall. If you're on the Camino, you'll be walking, experiencing the world at the speed of a human. You may be doing all of the above. Embrace and enjoy every part of your experience.

Pilgrimage is a quest for self; it is about the renewal of the soul and a desire to have a life well lived. With each step, every mile, each encounter you go deeper into yourself to find that meaning, to live the more authentic life you desire, to have no one to please or be accountable to but yourself. This is where you find the essential traits that pilgrims need: Flexibility to change plans, to stop at the unexpected, to go with the flow, a willingness to help your fellow travelers, to step outside your needs and desires, strength to hold your tongue and endure discomfort, courage to speak a foreign language, to try new foods and even ride a horse up a mountain, awareness that you have come to be transformed by the world, every part of it.

A pilgrim pays attention to the surroundings. It is time to notice the details of the world around you. You are traveling to see and feel for yourself, to personally see the world and know. It is a time to put down books and ideas and feel, sense what the world has to tell you, what you need to learn. For every encounter has meaning. When you are working in accordance with the natural world and your heart, the world rises to meet you. You've entered a place outside of time and space that is only for the soul, to experience the Divine directly.

This is the time to find compassion for yourself; you may be struggling with the rigors of travel or your own healing heart. When we find compassion for ourselves, we open the compassion for others that we meet. It is compassion that opens up the heart to let transformation work magic in your life. Let go of expectations and have compassion for your life, those you love or who have harmed you and those that fate has put in your path on this special journey. This is part of getting out of your head and into your heart, the more you enter the heart the more you see the divine in everything.

How will you remember these experiences? How can you breathe it into you body? It is important not to put anything between you and this new world, but as humans, we like to record our lives. Photographs are the most common way of remembering. But how many times I have seen people taking pictures and not experiencing. They only see the beauty through a tiny lens. Unless your purpose there is to take pictures, take just the ones you need to help your memory, to record the moment. Another way to help focus your experience is to concentrate on a topic. One trip to Egypt I became fascinated by the hands on the carvings of the gods. I took pictures of just hands as they express love, worship, and conflict. In Spain, I focused on farm animals and flowers. In England, I couldn't get enough of stones and trees. What fascinates you on your journey?

Journaling is also a way to capture the moment. Recently I came across my grandfather's log of his month-long journey to Europe in 1962; a detailed report of his voyage on a ship and all of the experiences in a world he never expected to see. He died a few years later, and it is so special to have his words and handwriting. Although there are many books on journaling, find the method that works for you. This is your private account and there to help you focus on what you have learned. On the Camino, I would take just a few pictures of the most important part of the day and notice things I wanted to remember. The next morning when I would wake up before I got out of bed,

I would choose five pictures and write about 500 words to remember that day. It was just the right amount to highlight the trip to my friends and family, but my own mind could fill in much more detail about the day. When you're on a long trip, the days can run together, and a simple reminder helps focus the individual experiences.

It is time to leave your expectation and let the journey show you what you need to know and experience. Expectations—preconceived ideas of what you want or think will happen—leave no room for serendipity. Serendipity is where the divine finds you, where you receive the blessings that can't be planned or anticipated. I always find that the moments of openness hold the joy and the help that you need. A prayer for help when I was lost brought a couple in a car to get me back on track. A little kitten in a garden reminded me of the innocence and gentleness that softens the hard edges of life. Bad weather can bring an afternoon in a tea shop to relax and read the perfect poem. A power outage means a night full of stars with no artificial light to interfere.

Sometimes pilgrimages have times of absolute difficulty. Missed planes and delays, lost passports and credit cards, injuries and illness. I had to find a doctor in Burgos, Spain for my daughter who had a sinus infection that desperately needed antibiotics. I have been on a tour when one of our fellow travelers died unexpectedly in the night from a heart defect. On my trips to Egypt in 2011, the Egyptian Revolution began, and my fellow travelers and I were confined to our hotel for several days until we could get flights out of the country. Hopefully, none of these things will happen on your journey. Just remember that every part of your pilgrimage has a lesson for you, one you need and want to learn whether you planned for it or not.

Most journeys don’t entail a huge calamity, but they all come with a certain amount of frustration and discomfort. Don't be afraid of the discomfort, don't think the discomfort is a failure. If you want only ease and comfort, then pilgrimage is not for you. The nature of pilgrimage is to grow your life in a new direction, and growth comes with hard work, pain, discomfort, disappointment. But it also comes with the reward of a life fully lived and the knowledge that you came to be more. Your trials and tests help you find a place of personal and spiritual power. Your effort and desire transform you.

One mistake I’ve watched some pilgrims make is comparing their journey and destination to their home. You have traveled to experience another culture and open yourself to a new world. It isn't going to be home---that is the whole point. Each land and culture have unique perspectives and unique gifts. By comparing and judging you lose the chance to be open and learn and understand. You have traveled to see the world differently than a tourist; you have come to see what others don't see—the divinity in everyone and everything.

Arrival

THE MOMENT HAS COME, and you are at your destination. The call, preparation, and journey have led you to the long-dreamed-of sacred site. Your holy place is the bridge between conscious and unconscious, the in-between place where you can touch the Divine.

On my Camino journey, the final destination seemed so far away that I rarely thought about it. I focused on that night's hostel or the goal for the next day. About a week before I arrived in the holy city of Santiago, it started to feel real. The last day of walking was a mix of anticipation and sadness that my walk would soon be over. I loved the walking so much that, in some ways, I didn't want it to end, but I was tired too. The moment we walked up to the cathedral was exhilarating. We did it, 500 miles in 5 weeks! We stood in line to get our certificates to prove we walked, and while waiting, we saw many of our pilgrim friends. The next few days in Santiago were a big celebration. We went to Mass, where our home country and starting point were read. We reunited with our friends and ate dinner and exchanged stories and lessons. We explored the city and the cathedral. I spent a lot of time in the cathedral during Mass and when it was quiet. I needed time to process my pilgrimage. When my friends arrived with a suitcase of clothes, I was not ready to wear them. I was not ready to take off my pilgrim clothes. I did all of the pilgrim rituals: went to see the casket of bones, went behind the altar to touch the statue of Saint James, and watched the Botafumeiro, the giant incense burner fly through the cathedral billowing smoke while the nun sang a special song. I had arrived, and I wanted to enjoy every bit. I was a pilgrim, and I was in Santiago.

When that moment comes for you—when the bus or car has pulled into the parking lot and there before you is the stone circle, cathedral, pyramid, temple, the mountain you have longed for—take a deep breath of thanksgiving. It can be overwhelming, and it might be different than you imagined. There can be tears or just quiet joy and wonder. Sometimes when I get to my destination, all thinking just stops. My conscious mind is on overload. It can be a challenge to stay present; the energy can be so overwhelming. Accept that your reaction is right for you. Use all your senses to feel, hear, touch, smell and see the magic.

Take those first few minutes to stop and take it in. There's no need to rush. Your site has been there a long time. At specific sites I like to take almost a ceremonial approach. For the temples in Egypt, I would slowly walk down the entrances which were often lined with sphinx, wondering, How did the people before me arrive at this space? I like to walk through the whole space slowly and systematically to take in every aspect and corner. I walk in silence with devotion. If I'm talking or taking pictures that the first moment of wonder can be missed.

Some sites you will relate to more than others. It is just fine if you don't make a connection to a site. Don't be disappointed if you don't. Not every site holds what you need. Sometimes you connect with a place that you never expected to or come on a site that touches your heart and wasn't even in your plan. This is all the magic of the pilgrimage that your heart and mind are open to the unexpected joy.

Come to this time with great simplicity of spirit and humility.
Find your inner stillness.

Sometimes it isn't easy to find this stillness. Fellow pilgrims, tour guides, tourist, merchants are all mixed into the site, but you don't have to let them keep you from your work. Your job is to connect and communicate with the site.

Give the site time to greet you, too. A sacred site is a combination of universal forces, sacred energy, veneration, and prayers. You have come to interact with the place, the memories and wisdom there. You alone are enough. Your presence and devotion are all you need. You enter the energy and history of the space to come in alignment with the subtle energies. It is fine if you don't feel anything or make a conscious connection, your body and heart know and understand what the mind can't always take in.

After all, our bodies are the medium our souls work with. When we stand physically in a spot that holds the memories of millennia or in a stunningly beautiful place, we are combining our exterior form and the interior into one transcendent form. This is a sacred space that supports the spiritual life. Once you have stood in these places, asked for more, and said words of thanksgiving, these places never leave you. You always have that moment to return to for the rest of your life. These experiences, for they are longings of the soul, will inform the rest of your life.

Now it is time to get down to the more conscious work of communicating with the site. You are not here to change this holy place but to have it change you. I've known people to visit sites to "fix" the energy, complaining that it is off or not right. Believe me; these sites need no fixing. They have been there long before you and will continue long after you are gone. When you visit a site with devotion and a desire to grow, you will be able to tap into the essence of the site. This is when you bring your gifts to contact with the divine. Maybe you will bring the traditional offering of tobacco or flowers, say a prayer of thanks, sing or listen to a song to connect music with the experience. You can find a quiet place for meditation or read a sacred scripture. I like to pray for those I love, speaking their names to connect them to the sacredness of the place.

When you are at a sacred place, you are also in sacred time. Time expands beyond your usual daily routine, and your memory becomes heightened. You might not remember what happened last Tuesday, but you will remember the day you stood in your first cathedral. The awe of the experience never leaves you. This sacred time is really time standing still for you to be in this holy moment.

This is the way to give to this holy place as well as receive the blessing and wisdom. This is the way you interact and communicate with the sacred. As you have made an effort and sacrifice to be at this place you have become more open to the subtleties of this interaction. These are "thin" places where the divine shines through.

Return

IT IS NOW TIME to return home. It is hard to leave the place that you longed for not knowing if you will ever see it again. Bless the place and thank it for the experience. There is a sense of sadness that the journey is over, you have dreamed of your quest for so long that it can be a shock that it is finished and you are in your own bed again. But without the return home, it wouldn't be a pilgrimage. You must complete the circle, return with new wisdom. The sacred journey and the return home are equally important.

My Camino journey was seven weeks long, a very long time to be away from home. It seemed like I would never be home. Yet, I did go home. The first month was a bit of a shock to reenter my life. I had to recover from jet lag, sort out the house, clean up the office work that was neglected but more importantly try to make sense of what I had just done. I needed time in my own space to just be with my experience. I came home with so much uncontainable joy that every moment of being home was infused with my pilgrimage.

When you cross the threshold of your front door, you are no longer a traveler. Thank the Divine for your safe return. End your journey with a ritual, take your time and just sit with being back in your home. Your friends and family will be happy to have you home and may want you to get right back to things, but you have changed, and you need time just to be. The change may be significant, like a big decision, or it may be subtle like a new attitude or more introspection.

Be gentle with yourself, try to build a little buffer to your return. You will have laundry and mail and the life you are used to, but you have changed. Your friends and family might only be interested in the highlights or not interested at all in your travel experience. You may feel very alone on your return. That's okay. You're not finished yet.

The call of the pilgrimage is actually a call to the home of our authentic self. It is home where you get down to the day to day work of living a spiritual life. The goal is to make you feel more at home, more integrated into life. I came home from a pilgrimage to England more content with my life in Tennessee. I had longed for England, and when that longing was satisfied, then I appreciated home more deeply. You must return to where you belong, where you feel safe and nurtured. The call of the journey is strong, but the return to home is calling now too.

Know that your journey is not over, travel is a powerful tool for your spiritual growth and to recreate your life. This is the first step in integrating the changes that you have asked for. Home is where we integrate our experiences. We didn't go on a pilgrimage to escape but to grow and make greater connections with our world, our life and others.

Home is the true destination. To return home transformed by the journey is the real pilgrimage. You have returned with a new consciousness. You have returned your new best self back to the world, and, really, all you have to give to the world is yourself. When the time is right, you will hear another call and take another journey.

Integration

BIG JOURNEYS AND BIG EXPERIENCES take time to settle into your life. The changes may come swiftly or take time to integrate. Pilgrimage is grounded, a physical spirituality that infuses all parts of your life from what decisions you make to how you react to the difficulty and details of everyday life. When you return home, you have to take the time to reorder your life to reflect the new self and the new way you see others. The spiritual and the material world come together as a new way of life.

On the Camino, I asked to be strengthened by the experience. I don't think my family and friends would have described me as a weak person, but there were some life experiences that I had not faced that scared me. Within a few weeks of returning home, I faced the personal challenges that I had always feared, confrontation and death. I had to confront a family member who was betraying the family, and my father was diagnosed with terminal cancer. My newfound strength gave me the courage to face these trials. Before I would have avoided these situations and found places to hide or denied my feelings. But with my new found strength I was able to confront my fears head-on.

The winter after my pilgrimage my father and mother came to my house to stay. The hospice nurses came weekly; my brother moved in, many family members came to say goodbye. My father and I sat together those two months walking our own personal interior pilgrimage together until it was time for him to cross over. Through it all, my new strength didn't fail me as I faced the sad emotions that I always avoided. I was so grateful to my pilgrimage for giving me that gift so I could be there for my family.

There will be the changes you have asked for, sometimes neither fun nor comfortable; growth isn't always easy. But staying the same and just going through life on autopilot is no way to live. Safe isn't what you asked for, so don't be surprised when things, people, places, and ideas leave, allowing new ones to take their place.

After my first trip to Egypt, I thought everything would be the same when I got home. I had no idea how to integrate that life-changing pilgrimage. On this journey, I had asked for more...and I got it. I was blindsided as my entire life was shaken by dear friends who left my life quickly and I had no idea why. No one had told me that intense dedication to move your life forward means you will never be the same. So be sure you understand what you are really asking for and be prepared to receive it, and everything that comes with it.

New and wonderful opportunities will also come with this devotion to your growth. Life can be happier and more fulfilling. A new peace comes along with gratitude for life. New doors open and your life can change directions in ways you never imagined. You may have had preconceived ideas about the pilgrimage, but then you find the journey was about something you never expected or considered. New teachers or new avenues of work or study may reveal themselves. These may catch you entirely by surprise and affect your life's path. Don't be afraid to follow this new direction.

The transformative nature of a pilgrimage teaches you to be, who you are. Not what you should do but "who you are." Purpose comes from knowing your authentic self. You see your life with more spiritual power and connection. Over time you uncover the person you have always been. You have the rest of your life to live this truth. Your deeper authentic self— has learned to be at home no matter where you are.

Part 2

Forty day Pilgrimage

Introduction

I WAS ONLY A FEW WEEKS AWAY from the beginning of my Camino journey, and I was doing what so many Americans do on Easter weekend—watching "The Ten Commandments." I had seen the movie many times before and was only half watching it. My upcoming journey was on my mind, and I was a bit overwhelmed by the sheer length of the pilgrimage— around 40 days. That's a long time to be away from home, a long time to walk and a long time to be faced with the continual unknown. But Moses' journey was 40 years in the wilderness. Maybe mine wasn't so long after all.

I started to think of the many times the number 40 was used in the Bible. The flood was 40 days and 40 nights. Moses spent 40 days on Mount Sinai before receiving the Ten Commandments. Jesus was in the wilderness 40 days while the Devil was tempting him. 40 days after Jesus' resurrection he ascended. Lent is the 40 day period of fasting and prayer preceding Easter. Then I started thinking of other times the number 40 is significant. Mohammad spent 40 days fasting and praying in a cave. According to an Arabic proverb, 'to understand people, you must live among them for 40 days.' In our natural world, human gestation is 40 weeks. The planet Venus returns to its original point in the night sky every 40 years.

There is something about the number 40 that makes the time extraordinary. It is an expansive period of time that takes a real physical and psychological commitment. In our fast-paced world, the idea of taking forty days to reflect on life seems unfathomable to most. That is more than a month and crosses the usual 30-day billing cycles that currently control our lives. There is a level of complication to such a long period of time. Most people are lucky to have a week or maybe two of time off every year from everyday work and then it is filled with obligations to family and friends.

The sad truth is, often without an extended period of time to open our hearts and minds, changes that we need to make simply won't happen. Time expansion creates the space to allow the mind, body, and heart to change direction. We are so used to deadlines, clocks, alarms, and schedules that a day without time commitments is unimaginable. When my children were young, my life revolved around school pick-up time. Everything had to come to a halt so I could be in a specific place at a particular time. My favorite days of the year were our annual vacation to the beach when there were no clocks, no pick-up, no routine. The deep relaxation that comes with following your desires and body rhythms is like a tonic to take away the stress of life. When you take an expansive length of time to commit to the desires of your heart and soul, then you open the space for the Divine to move in, and you live your life in alignment with the heart rather than the unconscious world.

A few days before I left for Spain, I had lunch with my friend Val. In addition to being the final days before I was to travel into the unknown for nearly seven weeks, it was also my 50th birthday. As a gift, she gave me a little pink net bag containing handwritten cards. Each card had a thought for the day. She had made these cards so she could feel connected to my journey. Val was meeting me in Santiago, and we were going to travel in Spain together for another week. These cards were meant to help me find a connection with each day. These special cards are the inspiration for this book.

Each day builds on the day before, each week on the week before, as you take each experience to the next level. After the first three weeks, you take what you have learned and experienced and apply it to your expanding life. These 40 days are a template for you, to make your journey meaningful to you and give you context for what it means to be a human living a full life on this earth. So here are suggestions for making this pilgrimage work for you. It is unrealistic and unnecessary to expect everyone to leave home for the full 40 days. But I encourage you to commit this expanded time, this sacred time, to your soul's growth.

You can take the 40 days in your own home, committing time every day to contemplation and prayer, walking and reading. Maybe taking some shorter trips to places that are meaningful or you have always wanted to visit. You can also designate a special place to go to every day as part of your sacred internal pilgrimage. Clear your calendar of commitments and choose to spend time alone. Consider opening your time by not watching TV or using internet for entertainment. This is a sacred time for you to examine your life.

Your 40 days can also include a physical journey. You can start your journey with a pilgrimage and expand the experience by finishing the 40 days at home with extra time to reflect and integrate your experience. You can also start the journey, setting your intentions, with a period of reflection to prepare for your physical pilgrimage, take the pilgrimage and finish the 40 days reflecting and integrating. Your journey could also come at the end of the 40 days as a culmination of the preparation you started weeks before and as a grand finale of this sacred time. You get to choose what works for you and your life.

Week 1

Finding

Day 1 - Finding Security

As you take your first steps on your journey so many emotions come to the surface; excitement, anticipation, joy, and fear, too. For you are stepping into the unknown both in the physical world and in your own internal, private world. You don't know what you will find or experience, and that is scary. Moving into a wider world brings up so many questions. What if you miss your flight? Do you have the stamina for the journey? What if you get sick or something happens to you or your family? These thoughts go round and round in your mind for you are leaving the security of your everyday life.

The unknown is frightening, but what is even more frightening is a world left unexplored, and personal potential left unrealized. As you take the first steps on your pilgrimage remember why you are taking this deeply personal and spiritual journey. You heard the Call and felt the soul's desire to answer.

I think the important first step of facing your fear and anxiety is laying the foundation for your journey. Examine what frightens you most. Is it leaving home? The journey? What will you find there? Or are you worried that you have spent time and money to find nothing? Journeys always hold a bit of risk as you travel to a foreign place, but you need to trust that you are a pilgrim for a reason.

As I have stepped out into the unknown on a long journey, I have learned to trust myself and my plans. I have done the best I can to make sure I've not made foolish choices that will put me in harm's way. This is not about blindly believing you will be magically protected; it's about trusting yourself enough to know that you can handle what comes your way. That is ultimately the strength and empowerment you are seeking. This is the time to remember why you answered the Call, to know and experience the divine in your life. You have the tools and resources to make your pilgrimage meaningful and blessed no matter what.

The first day of my Camino pilgrimage was filled with plenty of anxiety. I had 24 hours of travel on four different modes of transport to get to the starting point of my walk. There was so much that could have gone wrong, but every step of the way I reassured myself that I could do this and that if something went wrong, I would find a way to fix it. And so can you. You are meant to be on your journey, and you are capable of handling whatever arises.

Day 2 - Finding Happiness

Our desire as humans to find happiness became an inalienable right when the Thomas Jefferson wrote his famous introduction to the Declaration of Independence. Before then, happiness was not considered one of the most important goals of human existence. Never before had the average human had the freedom to follow their inner dreams and desires. We don't realize how revolutionary the idea of personal happiness was to the evolution of humans. No longer bound to just survival, the pursuit of happiness has taken humans to the next level of consciousness.

With the right to happiness comes the responsibility for happiness. Our happiness is not determined by a force outside of ourselves. Yes, it is easy to be joyful when life is going well, and the sun is shining, the children are behaving, and the bank account is adequate. But what about when life isn't perfectly rosy, which is often a majority of the time? What about when there is traffic, unexpected bills, you don't feel well, or someone is unkind?

Happiness isn't about being giddy all day long but a lightheartedness with life, a knowledge that despite the challenges of life there are blessings. Today is the day to make a physical or mental list of times you were happy or experiences that made you happy. What do these memories teach you about your personal happiness? Are you happy with your life now? What could you do to make yourself happier?

One of the goals of pilgrimage is to leave behind your burdens to make room for more joy and happiness to fill your life. This is how you withstand the ups and downs of life. You will need your personal happiness to draw on when times are tough, and there will be tough times on your pilgrimage. You'll need the happiness that is always inside of you, and you'll need to know how to draw it out when you need it most.

Day 3 - Finding Power

Every day of this first week you are setting a solid foundation for your journey of self-discovery. You are looking inside to find the most essential elements of a self-fulfilling life. Like happiness, if you constantly look outside yourself, you will always be at the whims and pressures of the world, and that will never work. Today it is time to examine your experience of power; when you have power, when others have power over you, and when you give away your power.

By power, I don't mean the ability to control others or have great influence in the world. I mean your personal, spiritual power. Finding your power is essential to finding and acknowledging those parts of your life that aren't working for you anymore. We are so constantly bombarded by advertising and politics, obligations and busy-ness that you may not be sure what your own thoughts and feelings really are. You may have people and situations in your life that have so much control over you that even the first step out is overwhelming.

I will say that just by accepting the Call and having the courage to step out on the path shows that you have found the beginnings of your own capabilities and confidence. A pilgrimage outside of your normal life helps loosen the grip of other people's opinions of your life and choices, and it brings that beautiful crack of mental space where your desires and dreams can find their first light in your mind.

So take a moment and see what has power and control over your life. Who do you give your power to? Who do you try to control and manipulate? This is the day to start being honest about your relationships where you unconsciously control or are controlled.

Don't worry if this makes you uncomfortable. If it does, that's proof you need the change that pilgrimage will bring. This is the first step in the process. Over the next 37 days, we will spiral back over the layers of your life to slowly unwind the elements that have kept you stuck, and you will replace them with your own deep knowledge of the Divine.

Day 4 - Finding Compassion

As you continue your steps forward on the journey to the heart of the Divine you have to begin examining your own heart. For ultimately this is a journey into the heart—the soul of your physical life on earth and the point where you connect to the divine.

But the place you start is the connection to your own self. Without compassion and acceptance for your own self, you won't have the strength or understanding to truly be compassionate in the world.

We tend to judge ourselves harshly, focusing on our mistakes, missteps, and problems. The first step to self-compassion is forgiveness for your past and what you regret. Take time to find a moment of tenderness for yourself and your mistakes. Regret is a strong emotion and can keep you chained to the past. Now you are on a journey to move forward and make new choices and find a deeper kindness for yourself, which ultimately leads to greater kindness for others.

I practice Buddhist Loving Kindness Meditation, and in this practice, you start by having loving-kindness for yourself and move outward. You are the center, and balance and harmony radiate out from you. The meditation begins with 'may I be healthy and strong.' This is starting with the body and acknowledging that you are a physical being and that without this physical body you wouldn't be able to take this remarkable journey in the world. Next, "may I be happy." Happiness allows us to enjoy life and be grateful for all the blessings of life. Then finally, "may I be filled with ease." When you can relax into life and leave worry behind, then you can fill your heart with the lightness of the divine. This is how we truly appreciate and enjoy our lives.

As you find compassion for yourself, then you breathe in and out these same prayers for those you love, those you feel neutral towards, those you have greater difficulty with and finally finishing with "may all beings everywhere be happy."

Finding universal compassion will not happen in a day and maybe not even in 40 days. But every day that you take a moment to forgive yourself and others will make it easier the next time hard feelings surface. There is much to forgive in this world, but each forgiveness is another stone set down from the burden you carry. Each time for you forgive gets you closer to a lightness of being.

Start simply.

What needs your forgiveness right now, in this moment?

What do you need to remove from your burden today?

DAY 5 - FINDING EXPRESSION

Throughout the process of pilgrimage, you are simultaneously adding new layers of experience to your external life and removing layers from your inner life, removing what you don't need and making space in your life for what you truly want. Dealing with emotions and finding a way to express your feelings is part of the many lessons on the journey.

Self-expression is a fine balance between being too closed off and oversharing. With the advent of social media, it is easy to overshare. You've also probably had the experience of denying or covering up your emotions, sometimes it's not to hurt others' feelings or because you need privacy. Suppressing strong emotions takes a lot of energy and can be very painful and, at times, very detrimental. Today, it is time to take a look at your feelings and see what needs to be expressed and find a healthy way to deal with strong emotions: happiness, sadness, joy, anger, embarrassment, fear, heartbreak. The act of taking yourself out of your ordinary environment and routine gives you time and space to feel and examine these emotions. There is a balance between denying emotions on the one hand and wallowing in the pain and hurt on the other. Use your spiritual journey to find the emotional and spiritual gold that lies in all human experiences.

We can't fix every issue quickly and easily, but each step on our 40-day journey moves us into new territory that puts us in a new place physically and emotionally, garnering perspective in our lives and our hearts. On your journey, I encourage you to write about your feelings, listen to music that brings you joy, take a picture of a moment of pure beauty, or say a prayer of gratitude when it feels right.

The first temple I visited in Egypt was Dar El-Bahari, the magnificent temple of the only female pharaoh, Hatshepsut. The temple has multiple levels all nestled against a giant mountain. The moment I started up the stairs, I unexpectedly found strong emotions welling up. I'm not sure I could even describe how I felt. All I knew was that this great temple touched some unnamed deep space in me. When I looked at this sacred temple, all I could do was sob. I had no idea why. I saw this unexpected outpouring of emotions again and again in my fellow travelers. You never know what sacred site will trigger these deep emotions, but, when it happens, the experience is powerful and undeniable. Some things must be expressed because they are the truth. You will find what needs to be expressed in you.

Day 6 - Finding Wisdom

My teacher always told me that wisdom is knowledge applied to life. We all have known wise people, the ones who seem to have an insight into life that takes us by surprise. Usually, wise people speak gently and lovingly because wisdom has taught them that kind words go deeply into the heart without resistance.

Today, look deep into your heart where wisdom lies and find some of the truths that have helped shape your life. Did they come from a grandmother or a book? Wisdom can be found in the most simple moments of life or in the most profound spiritual teachings. It can be found deep in your heart. If you take the time to listen, you will begin to hear the wisdom of your own inner voice.

There is an ambiguity to wisdom. Sometimes you get the answers you seek; sometimes you don't. Sometimes, you have to let the questions go and live the mystery of life.

Here are a few ways to access the wisdom inside you. First, begin with an open and loving heart. Just allow your heart to be open. It's as simple as that. When you do this, you will feel vulnerable. This may make you uncomfortable, but this is how you allow entrance to your soul's desire. Next, have an observant mind. Notice what is around you and what has been put in the path in front of you. Really take a look at everything that makes up your life. Take the time to stop and notice the flowers and trees, listen to the wind, and pick up the random book on the table. The more you connect, the more you will notice clues that lead you through the mystery of your life.

The most important part of finding your wisdom is the willingness to follow your own path. The well-trod path offered by the world will give you the same results that everyone else has, and you have asked for more. You have asked for your authentic life. So you must be willing to receive I and to live it.

When you do these three things, you will find that wisdom has been in you and around you all along.

Day 7 - Finding Consciousness

So many days we go through on autopilot. We drive our cars to familiar places, not sure of how we got there. We cook the same dinner over and over. Most of our lives are about routine. We seem to be working on a dream. One of the many reasons to be on a pilgrimage is to arise from the waking dream. By being in a new place and asking new questions, we expand our minds as we begin to see the world differently. We are seeking a new level of consciousness.

When we volunteer for this mission, we ask to leave old

parts of ourselves that no longer serve us or have been taken from us. We ask to go and find new aspects of ourselves to cope with our changed circumstances, open up new opportunities or reach higher levels of understanding. The challenges bring new strengths and experiences to drive this new level of consciousness.

The guides along the way are intuition and synchronicity (meaningful coincidences). We use our intuition, our gut feeling, to guide us and synchronicity to reassure us that we are on the right path. It is these two guides that brought us on this journey and will help us find what we are seeking.

Synchronicities become more common when we are in a time of emotional intensity or personal transformation. They are the little nudges that show us the next thing and bring us to the right place at the right time for our next experience and encounter. As we become more focused on waking up and leaving behind our inauthentic life, synchronicities become for frequent. Synchronicity and authentic life go hand in hand.

What has your intuition been telling you this week? Where are the synchronicities pointing?

Week 2

Activating

Day 8 - Activating Security

In the middle ages, pilgrimages were very dangerous endeavors. Pilgrims were taken advantage of by thieves at every turn. A Puente La Reina, Spain a noblewoman built a bridge for the pilgrims to Santiago just to protect them from the thieving ferrymen. Most modern pilgrims don't have such security problems. There is always the chance of losing a wallet or twisting an ankle, but the vast majority of travel is safe for us physically. But what about our mental and spiritual safety?

When we embark on a pilgrimage, we set out through unknown territory, and we need to keep our senses alert. We know that we are called to this experience, but we still have fear. The truth is, most of our fear comes from our thoughts and feelings. We lay awake at night worried not about our physical safety but our finance, relationships, loved ones, and our self-worth.

Today you need to know that the security you seek is internal and that to feel safe, you must accept that you are in the right place, right now. In other words, you have to trust your journey.

Pilgrims on the Camino talk every day about "Camino Miracles," times when the Way rises up to meet you, and your fellow pilgrims are perfectly placed for what you need. My daughter Alexandra couldn't decide which shoes she wanted for the long walk on the Camino. She bought an expensive pair of trail runners at the last minute, but she only wore them a few times before going back to using her thinner soled shoes. One afternoon she saw someone limping barefoot into town. His hiking boots had made horrible blisters on his feet, and his backup pair of sandals were now broken. He had no money to buy new shoes, and he couldn't carry on without them. Alexandra pulled out her extra trail runners, and, wouldn't you know it, they fit him perfectly. It seemed she had carried them all along just for this moment.

Pilgrimage is a journey of faith. If you trust in Divine protection, then you will experience it.

Day 9 - Activating Happiness

I was sitting at the edge of the known world in Abu Simbel, Egypt. Before me was one of the greatest temples ever built, with mammoth gods inside and out saying to the world: "This is the greatest kingdom the world has ever seen." I was in pure bliss. Everything in my vision was absolutely perfect. Then a pretty American woman came and sat down beside me and said, "It would look so much better if they would fix the front". It was a great lesson in perception. We see what we choose to see, experience what we want to experience.

You make your world happier if you choose to see the magic.

It is time to take a deeper look at your personal happiness. Not the happiness that you get when serving others and seeing their happiness, but your own personal true happiness. Pilgrimages by nature have plenty of difficult moments—physically, mentally and spiritually—but they also have moments of complete happiness. When you are miles away from the bank, post office, grocery store or laundromat, those worries and duties can be set aside. You can access the pure joy of being.

It is a day to focus on the little things of life, the moments of pure joy. When we are constantly focused on the big picture or finding greatness in our everyday life, we miss the flashes of happiness that is all around all the time. Our world is glorious, and as a pilgrim, you are reaching for that glory on a spiritual level. Look around today and find the glory and inexplicable moments of pure joy that the day brings. List them and see that just being aware of them turns them from little moments into continuous happiness. True personal happiness doesn't dwell in the big moments, but in appreciating and loving all the little moments life has to offer.

Day 10 - Activating Power

Now that you are past the first few challenging and exciting days of your pilgrimage, it is time to look again at personal power and what that means to you. Do you feel balanced in your personal power? Would you say that you don't have enough personal power? Do you feel like a doormat with people walking over you and your needs and desires? Or do you feel the need to control people and situations all the time?

Neither of these scenarios is a power that is balanced and working for you. Either you are showing not enough power or too much power. A lack of personal power is debilitating as your needs aren't getting met and you feel used and undervalued. Too much controlling power makes people fearful of you, and you will lack genuine balanced relationships.

When you activate your personal power in a balanced way, you find compromise and common ground. You speak up and ask for what you need. You don't stomp down your feelings as if they don't matter. If you are being used and pleasing people you will need great strength to overcome this pattern. You might need some professional help to encourage your new way of interacting with people. Breaking these personal patterns are one of the reasons why you are taking this pilgrimage--to live your authentic, balanced life.

If you prefer to control others and your environment at all times, then you are dealing with the other side of the same issue. On a pilgrimage, you have to loosen your control, let the path take you where your soul needs and not where your personal agenda wants. Some of the happiest moments traveling are when the unexpected shines through.

True personal power comes from knowing who you are and what you need while at the same time being aware of others' needs. When you activate your personal power, you'll find you can get along in the world much more harmoniously.

Day 11 - Activating Compassion

As you have traveled over a week now, how are you feeling about the hurtful moments of your life? Is the pain that others have caused you still in the forefront of your mind? Are you still replaying these painful words or situations over and over in your mind, making the story even more deeply grooved into your heart?

Activating compassion is part of the process of moving forward and living the new story. A hard part of being a pilgrim is leaving behind burdens and stories that cause you suffering. It is time to unwind some of those experiences and stories that have your heart so bound up. It is time to free these experiences and let them float away.

First, take the minor stories and remember them. Let them have one last hold on you. This is where we get to activate compassion for those who hurt us, situations that wounded us. Consider that others wound us out of their own traumas and brokenness. As we let go of that first tight thread around our heart, then the next one becomes easier to loosen, and then another thread can be unraveled until your heart is free. This takes time, especially if these stories have become woven into your identity. But you are changing your identity through this process to one of personal power and courage and love. You are on the path to find greater meaning in your life and one that requires the unbinding of your past.

The last night I was in Santiago I had dinner with some fellow pilgrims, some of whom I hadn't met before. We talked about our experiences and what it meant to us. One older gentleman had a particularly tough time. He had been sick and injured and finally had to give up just before finishing; he just couldn't go on. In his broken state, he finally had a breakthrough with his heart. He realized that his father, who had long passed away, had been suffering from PTSD, which was not diagnosed or treated in those days. His father had unknowingly passed this trauma to his son, who was still suffering 50 years later. This realization of this transferred trauma gave my fellow pilgrim the clarity and strength to forgive his father. In tears, this man shared with me that he had finally released this pain and found the compassion for his father he had been looking for. Earlier that day the office where he was to receive his certificate of completion heard his story and gave him a Compostella, the official certificate, for his efforts. This man had walked more miles than anyone…in his heart. He had unbound his broken heart and walked now in compassion. When I last saw him, he was headed home to repair his relationship with his own children, whom he had unintentionally traumatized with his inherited pain.

Forgiveness and compassion are unbelievably powerful for transformation. No matter what has happened to you in the past, you can be free from it. Now is the time to give life to the compassion in your heart and to let go of the pain that is holding you back.

Day 12 - Activating Expression

One of the tools for pilgrims to fully experience the journey is openness; to cultivate an openness to the experience, the joys, hardships, emotions, fears, and fellow pilgrims. This is difficult at times since society and family tell us to be guarded lest we get hurt physically and emotionally. But without letting in these new experiences and places and people, how will you expand your life?

The shared journey allows for an openness with other pilgrims that is rarely experienced in regular daily life. When you meet other pilgrims on the way, you immediately have common ground, a common goal that makes open conversation more natural. You share your motivations, your homeland, your call to the journey and your story. You find out things about others and their lives very quickly. This is the time when an openness about our thoughts and feelings is easier and feels safer. The common experience provides a connection.

The newness of each day provides openness in your own heart to find new joys, excavate old wounds, make new discoveries and forge a new path to the Divine. That feeling of laying yourself bare to what is around and inside feels a bit scary, but that is the whole point of stepping out into new territory. Courage is part of this openness, the courage to be vulnerable and to acknowledge your feelings.

The openness and willingness to make new friends and share my life with my fellow pilgrims have been one of the biggest blessings of my journeys. Sometimes these connections are just for a conversation or a moment of help. But other times it is a meeting of lifelong friends. I have become dear friends with people around the world, people I could never have met in ordinary life. After my second trip to Egypt, one of my new friends from Australia came and stayed with me for a month. We had read the same books, had similar goals, spoke the same spiritual language. We would have never found each other in any other circumstance yet we had so much in common. Our willingness to be open gave us a friendship that was special and rare.

You have no idea who may be on their way to meet you at this very moment. By allowing yourself to be open, being willing to express and share yourself with others, the Universe finds a way to connect you to exactly who you need. Are you ready to invite them into your life ?

Day 13 - Activating Wisdom

Everyone has inner vision, but most days there is too much noise in our environment actually to see and hear our inner vision and voice. The inner voice is the part of us that already knows what to do and what is right for your life and soul. This is the time to get back in touch with your inner knowing, your discernment.

Discernment is the ability to make a good decision for yourself and your life. Without discernment, you are buffeted by those around you and their needs and desires for you. It seems that everyone knows what is best for you or wants something from you. Discernment is the ability to say "this is for me or this is not for me."

Discernment doesn't always follow everyday logic. I have felt the call to pilgrimages that don't make much sense to my practical nature. In 2011 I felt very called to go to Egypt for the third year in a row. My practical self—said that I had already been twice and I didn't need to spend the money, but my heart said I must go. Thank goodness I listened, it was a very powerful trip ending in a front row seat to the Egyptian revolution. I was meant to be there.

Another time a friend invited me to go to Scotland, a place I just love. My mind said that is was a great idea and a perfect opportunity. But my heart said the timing wasn't right; I just didn't feel it was the right choice. It was a good thing I listened because my family needed me during that time and I would not have been able to go to Scotland. I didn't know why I wasn't feeling called to that trip at the time, but I was glad I had listened to my intuition.

Society is also happy to cover up your inner voice with the pressures of materialism, what you should do and be to make your life fit in nice and easily with everyone else. The decision to go on a pilgrimage says that you want to step out of society and its demands for a time and find that quiet inner voice. The whole process of a pilgrimage is to align your inner vision with your outer life.

Today is a day to remember and move toward what you know your life is missing or your heart's desire. Listen to your inner voice.

That inner knowing is there to guide you, to lead you to the experiences and places that best align with your soul's calling.

Day 14 - Activating Consciousness

Today you have been on your journey for two weeks, and the rhythm should be more natural. Much has happened already, and you can already look back on what you have experienced and learned. But most of all I hope that your experiences will be something you reflect on and bring new insight to your life.

On your journey to transformation and healing, you are starting to have some insight into the true nature of life. Insight is part of the discernment process for finding the underlying truth of your life. Not only do you learn what is you and what is not you, but insight adds the layer of why this is true.

Transformation is about seeing the world and yourself differently, but this isn't possible without the gift of insight into your thoughts and actions. Your past way of being and experiencing the world has brought you to this point, and now it is time to examine how these past experiences are limiting your view of life.

We are essentially connected to the limitless universe. That is our true identity. However, society, religion, family, trauma, and other things can instill in us a self-identification that limits the true experience of the individual's oneness with the Divine. The roles we play in life become so real to us that we identify with them, and we forget that our roles are just masks we wear in the world. Who are you without your roles? Who are you without your job, home, ethnicity or gender? At the core, we are pieces of the Divine and this journey you have been called to is to help you reconnect with your divinity.

Week 3

Expressing

DAY 15 - EXPRESSING SECURITY

When on a pilgrimage you will have days that make you wonder, "What was I thinking?" You will miss your warm bed and comfy couch. It is disorienting to have everything new; nothing is familiar or comfortable. What will you do when you feel overwhelmed by the day or your own emotions? This is when you find Trust.

Trust is a foundation stone of our life. It is essential to building relationships with others and with yourself. Today is the day for looking at trust in your life. We need reliability in our life and trust provides the reassurance that the creature comforts of life like food and water, shelter and love. When you take away that reliability how do you replace this trust in life?

The key is to trust yourself that your needs will be met. Trust in the good in your life and that what you have asked for in this journey will be for your greatest good and greatest joy. Trust in your own abilities to figure things out and that you have the internal resources to make the right decisions.

You wouldn't be on this journey if you didn't trust the call to the adventure. You need to find that trust that initially propelled you onto this path. It is there. You just have to tap into it. Every pilgrimage has its moments when trust is all you have, such as when you are physically lost. When the journey takes a different direction than you had initially planned, you have to trust that your experience will be perfect for your journey.

Trust your own inner strength to find the solution to problems. You need to trust your gut-instinct when you come to a crossroads. Listen to that feeling and trust yourself. Without trust, there is no way to have a relationship with a friend or family member, and you need to have that same relationship with yourself. You must trust what you know.

Originally I had planned to walk the Inca Trail in Peru. I was so excited to travel that famous walk to Machu Picchu. But a few weeks after I had booked the tickets I found out that the permits for the trail had fallen through. I couldn't change the airline tickets, so I looked into the alternate hikes that didn't require permits. Initially, I was very disappointed, but I knew I was meant to go to Peru. So I trusted that a different hike would be the experience I needed. I was right. The alternate trek, Lares Trek, was better suited for me. I loved the road less traveled and being with the local people in the small villages. I trusted the process and had the experience that was perfect for me.

DAY 16 - EXPRESSING HAPPINESS

When you have moments of true happiness, what does that look like to you? How do you feel when you are happy? Happiness is a state of well-being. Although life may not be perfect, you have a general feeling of contentment. For the moment, all is right in your world.

Happiness can be subtle and not always recognizable—a 'you don't realize what you have until it's gone' kind of thing. So let's make sure that happiness is an everyday part of your life, that you recognize the beautiful place in your heart that is the seat of well-being.

One of the most charming characteristics of happiness is curiosity. This joyful need to find out something about the world comes from a state of equinimity. Curiosity comes in the moments when the cares of the world do not weigh too heavy on you, so your mind has a moment to play and explore. This desire to know more can take you in delightful directions such as a walk down a winding path, in a labyrinth of internet searches, the opportunity to question an interesting person or a ramble in a library.

Bring curiosity into your adventure and see what you can discover. Maybe you're curious about food you've never tried or a small shop you passed by. Curiosity can occur at the lunch table with a fellow traveler as you dig deeper into the meaning and history of the place you are currently at.

When you are curious about life, you open up your creativity so you can see your life in a new way. Creativity is birthed from this need to know more and be more, and isn't that the point of your journey? My pilgrimages certainly have helped my creativity. I was not interested in writing. Not at all.

It wasn't something I felt I did well. But I wanted to share my experiences and the joy that they had brought to my life. When a friend wanted to interview me on a radio show, I was required to have a website. I had no idea how to start until another friend interviened and helped me establish a blog about my travels. Although it was not an easy process for me to write, I was able to tap into my imagination and self-expression, something I had never done before with words. My curiosity for the world and travel and sacred sites sparked my inspiration and had taken me down a new path that I would have never experienced. I can't wait for you to discover what's in store for you when you let your curiosity and creativity loose.

Day 17 - Expressing Power

It took courage for you to take a pilgrimage. Most people don't even know what that is or why you would want to go. I'm sure when you announced your intentions to go to a faraway place or take time to yourself you were met with blank stares and silence. Some people might have been supportive but others couldn't understand it at all or might have said you were selfish to take the time or spend the money. But you honored your Call and took that courageous step into the unknown of the world and yourself.

Each step of your journey will build your courage, even if you have moments of doubt. Little by little, one courageous moment at a time, you will get stronger. What will this newfound courage look like in your life? Hopefully, it will look like new and healthy choices for you mentally, physically and spiritually. You will make a strong commitment to your personal growth and make sure that your spiritual life gets nurtured every day.

Physically you will be strengthened and find the courage to try an experience you never knew you could do.

Emotionally I hope that your new courage will find its way into your relationships with friends, family, and partners. It is time to make the changes, subtle or great, that bring you into alignment with your personal integrity and that honor you and those you love. This is not the time to impose your will on others but to hold your own ground and build healthier relationships. Speak up for yourself without drowning out the other voices.

Personally, I hope your new courage includes responsibility for yourself and your choices. I hope you will be ready to pursue the things in life that bring you joy. What changes in your attitude and habits can you make to be a more productive and self-fulfilled person?

Day 18 - Expressing Compassion

As you have been on this journey, I hope that you have opened yourself and are enjoying the wonder of life and this amazing planet you live on. Curiosity, wonder, delight, creativity, trust, courage; these are the characteristics you are rediscovering in the core of your heart. I say 'rediscover,' because you discovered them the first time long ago. These are the characteristics that children naturally express. In our true nature is this same child-like nature that is open to life. In the heart of our true self is simplicity.

Simplicity is where the most elemental parts of our soul reside. When you come down to what is most important, it isn't all the things that society demands. At the core of simplicity is kindness, gentleness, openness. These are the places from which true joy radiates. It isn't about the bright lights and glamor of the world but about flowers and trees, waterfalls and stars. It is the part of our earth that is accessible to all.

This is the joy of a pilgrimage because it strips your life down to the most essential elements. A pilgrimage is about genuinely interacting with nature and other people and ultimately the Divine. When you go on a pilgrimage, you are asking for your life to be brought down to the simplest elements so that you can rebuild with new experiences and awareness. The Divine is the bright light that shines from each of our hearts, and sometimes you need to go into the world to find what you already have.

Day 19 - Expressing Yourself

Every one of us is a beautiful part of the Divine, a unique drop in the ocean of infinity. But how do you express your uniqueness? At the core of self-expression is your own knowing of exactly who you are. And how do you find that out? Through the process of self-reflection, you look at the parts of your life that make up the whole of your personality: your choices, your opinions, and preferences, your experiences and life-path.

You express your true self through your actions. I often say "I don't care what you believe, I care how you act." We have our different philosophies and ideas, but how you behave toward yourself and your fellow humans really shows your true nature. If I asked your closest family how they honestly feel about you, would you like what they say? Your actions are the expression of your true self.

Another way to bring some self-reflection into your journey is to examine your motivations. Why do you make the choices you do? Is it from your heart or out of fear? For personal gain or the interest of all? To please yourself or to please others? Why did you embark on this pilgrimage? This is a journey to the heart, and without discovering your deeper longings and motivations, the journey will bring superficial results.

This time of self-reflection really helps you get to the heart of personal expression. If your behavior comes from a lack of conscious reflection, then you are always acting without understanding the consequences. You repeat the same patterns of your life. This pilgrimage can help you change that if you all yourself to uncover the parts of yourself that you really want to shine. Because, for better or worse, the stress of traveling will reveal who you really are. I've watched people step up and lead in a difficult situation, and others give up when things get tough. I've seen many lose their cool over a flight delay, while just as many keep it together and go with the flow when challenged.

Take time today for introspection and self-reflection. Forgive when you have failed and know that this pilgrimage is meant to transform you into your truest self.

Day 20 - Expressing Wisdom

Have you ever been in the presence of a truly spiritual person? You just want to soak up the feeling you have when you are with them, bottle it and take it with you so you can keep relishing that experience of wisdom and love. I have a dear friend who, when I first knew her, made me want to hold her hand and cry because she radiated such a deep motherly love.

In order to be living the truth of your life, you need to see clearly what that truth is. What is the truth of your life? First, you must be honest about your values and desires. You might talk about valuing your family when in reality you make very little time for them. You might think that other people don't notice, but they do. Others know when you don't carry through with your word or say one thing and do the opposite. This all leads to an incongruent life. When parts of your life don't line up, there is no way to hide it. Your inconsistencies will show.

Pilgrimages are perfect for finding clarity. Taking the time to honor and grow your spiritual nature will bring the incongruent parts of your life to your attention. You can't become your truth if you are ignoring parts of yourself that are not compatible with that truth. Are you wanting a healthier life but still eating poorly and sitting on the couch too much? Do you want stronger relationships but tend to be crabby with your family? Do you want abundance in your life but waste your resources on needless things? Do you talk about your spiritual life but don't spend any time reading or praying?

As you live your truth and live every day being transparent with yourself about your motivations and choices, then your true self—shines bright, and others will notice that you are lighter.

Day 21 - Expressing Consciousness

Pilgrimages are times set aside to feel the joy and light of living and the beauty and wonder of our world. They are also times to reflect on loss and sadness that life inevitably brings. How do we balance the two? How do you enjoy life and mine the riches of everyday living when there are always sadness and tragedy in the world and in your life?

In between joy and sadness, there is stillness. In stillness, there is another world to be discovered. Have you ever experienced a moment when time stood still? Was it a moment when sorrow was all around but you knew you would go on? Or was it a moment of perfect beauty on a mountaintop or by the ocean or the birth of a child? Whatever it was, for that moment, you were outside of time—you experienced infinity.

Stillness is one of the gifts of pilgrimage. It might come when you are standing in the place you have longed for or when you know you are far away from home, and there is no going back. This is the amazing "ah-ha" moment in the journey which you might think comes with trumpets and fanfare, but really it is great peace opening up in your heart. Treasure that moment, feel it deeply, remember it, and then it will be easier to find in your daily life.

Stonehenge was high on my list of sacred sites to visit, but I didn't want my first encounter to be casual. I wanted that special moment. So when I was planning my trip to England in 2009, I made Stonehenge the starting point of that journey. I made special reservations to be at Stonehenge at sunrise and to be able to walk inside the stones, which is not allowed during regular hours. That morning, close to the autumn equinox, I arrived as the sun was rising over the Salisbury Plain. The guard checked my ticket, and I lined up with a few other people for the appointed time. The guard let down the chain, and I headed to those wise, ancient stones. I walked just a bit faster than the others because I wanted my moment alone in that circle. For just a minute or two, it was only the stones and me in the sunrise. It was a moment of perfect stillness; the feeling was gentle and pure. I knew I was home.

Week 4

Desires

Day 22 - Who Are You?

For the last 21 days, you have delved deeper and deeper into your life to uncover the gold that is your unique soul. You have gone searching to uncover happiness and security, power and love. Each week you looked closer into these core life principles and examined another layer of what these mean to your life. Now it is time to put them all together and ask the question, 'Who am I?'

It's a universal experience: that moment of looking in the bathroom mirror when you're not sure you recognize yourself. You wonder "who am I" "why am I here" "is this all" "what is my life about"? Pilgrimage is that journey of self-discovery that gives the time and space to reflect on the question of what your human life really means.

To the Western mind "who am I?" is usually a question of what do I do, where do I live, who am I related to, what do I own? These are the identifying markers our society sees as important and the way we evaluate where we stand in the hierarchy. They are the masks we wear in the world, and they don't even come close to answering the question.

You are a beautiful tapestry woven by your personality, soul, experiences, relationships, and desires. Everything about you is who you are, and yet at the center is Divinity. This is the you that you are searching for. The stillness of the Divine is the core of your being. As sons and daughters of the universe, we are all part of the greater experience of Life.

As you move into the next two weeks of the pilgrimage, you will move to recognizing and integrating your authentic nature. You will see who you are, not just in the material world, but in a relationship with the world, your fellow humans, the Divine, and, most of all, yourself. You will integrate the parts of your life. You will bring together the fragments of your personality and your soul to live the authentic life you so desire

Day 23 - Fearless You

It's highly likely that, on this journey, you have experienced moments of fear. It might be from physical danger, but it can also be as much about emotions, memories, and losses. Mostly we fear the unknown. Pilgrimage is about facing fears, real or imagined, and moving forward anyway. Courage is what we use to face our fears and to do the impossible.

Courage helps you face your fears and persevere even in the face of difficult, frightening or dangerous situations. Sometimes it is finding your strength to face an unpleasant task that stands in your way or a relationship that is holding you back. Courage gives you the conviction to act according to your values and beliefs despite facing criticism and resistance. Bravery, fearlessness, and courage are some of the pilgrim's tools. They keep you going and following your own path and heart.

Over the years I have had many fears. I feared confrontation and avoided it whenever possible, even if it meant giving up my needs and desires. On the Camino, I definitely felt that my courage was strengthened and I felt fearless with my accomplishment. My fearlessness was tested just a few short weeks after I returned home and had an intense confrontation with a family member. I faced one of my biggest fears and did what I needed to do. I know that before my pilgrimage I would have never been able to stand my ground in such a tense situation. I'd just walked across an entire country. I wasn't about to let someone walk over me.

Finding my fearless self—has been a joy and a strength to myself and my family. Where can being fearless improve your life and the lives of those you love? Are you willing to speak your truth? Are you willing to take a risk and go for an experience you have dreamed of? Will you go to school or start a business or confront a relationship that is not going well? I hope so. Because, if you are willing, these 40 days of pilgrimage will bring courage and clarity to your life.

Day 24 - Abundant You

If you are reading this book and taking a pilgrimage, if you have the time and energy to reflect on your inner life, then you are abundant. So much of the world's population is worried about their next meal and where they will be sleeping and their personal safety. After basic needs are met—clothing, food, shelter—our minds can turn to the deeper questions of meaning and purpose. These are the questions that have prompted your pilgrimage. These questions are the core of a bigger life. It is time to shift your view of abundance from material to spiritual wealth.

Our modern world has focused on material abundance for the last several hundred years. Since industrialization, our possessions have multiplied beyond what is useful or sustainable, yet still leaving us feeling empty and wondering "what now?"

I want to give you two new ways of bringing more abundance to your life. The first is gratitude; a practice that gives you an appreciation for the blessings already working in your daily life. We tend to focus on the things that are wrong with our lives instead of what is going well. Take a look at your life and be honest. I bet when you take an honest account of your life, you find that you have much more to be grateful for than you've been appreciating. In other words, count your blessings. By focusing on the gifts in your life rather than the lack, you will invite the abundance that you seek into your heart and your life.

Passion is another beautiful gift you have that will increase the abundance in your life. Passion brings with it enthusiasm, opportunities, joy and expanded experiences, the essence of spiritual abundance. What are you passionate about? What did you care about before 'real life' took over? These are the spirit-filled spaces where your life becomes fuller and more meaningful. If you've felt guilty or selfish about allowing yourself to 'indulge' in your passions, now is the time to stop. By allowing yourself to experience and live out your passion, you will discover a new facet of your life's meaning and purpose.

Day 25 - Empowered You

An important component of a pilgrimage is taking time out of society. This is the time to step away from the norms and demands of your current culture and take the time to see if society's values and your values are the same. You will be surprised how many assumptions you make about life because of your culture.

Leaving your familiar environment gives you room and time to really reflect on how you want to see and live life. Pilgrimage empowers you to live the life you desire. When you are empowered, you make the choices you know are right for your life, not the choices that the world imposes on you or that you make to please other people or keep the peace.

A pilgrimage strengthens you to make the authentic choices that bring meaning and joy to your life. Everyone is entitled to make the choices that are right for them. You don't need permission to live your life. Not everyone will be happy with your decisions, but you can call on your inner strength to hold your own against negative reactions. You might be called selfish or foolish because the people in your life would prefer you to stay as you are—the you they know is safe for them. But safe is not what you want.

How do you know if your choices are the right ones? How do you know your choices reflect your empowered self? Here are some clues; you aren't controlling others, you are happier, and so your life improves, others are happier around you because you radiate joy. When you raise your spirits, you naturally lift those who truly love you.

Making changes to empower your life may be subtle, or they may be very big. Sometimes it means moving, leaving a job or a spouse, but it can just as well be a change in attitude, a different outlook, a new way of relating to those you love. The changes may not be comfortable or fun, but doing what you always have done is no longer an option. You asked for more when you began the pilgrimage, now is the time to embrace what that request brings.

I had a history of choosing friends and relationships that were dominating. It was subtle, but I always played a submissive role. After my first pilgrimage to Egypt, I felt much more empowered although I wouldn't have necessarily used that term at the time. I had changed. I didn't even acknowledge it to myself, but the people in my life noticed. The changes in me caused a seismic reaction amongst my friends, and in a very short span of time, I lost them all. This experience shook me to my core, but ultimately it was for the best. Those people I'd thought my friends could not accept the new empowered me, and I wasn't going to go back into my submissive role in our relationships just to keep them. Since then, I have been blessed with more and deeper friendships than I could have possibly imagined at that time. Now my life is full of the people I truly need.

Today I challenge you not to hide from the changes you know you need to make in your life. You wouldn't have started this pilgrimage if you didn't want to make them. You've asked for more out of your life, so now it's time to face what that request brings.

Day 26 - Resilient You

The last three days we have uncovered the parts of who you are that build the foundation for your life. Without courage, personal power and abundant passion you can't have the resilience to have a life of peace and joy no matter what happens. Resilience is the knowledge that you can weather life's ups and downs and not lose yourself in the process. By adding these characteristics to your life, you can know you have built a firm and enduring foundation. If the winds of life continually blow you off course, then you won't be able to develop the consciousness and tranquility of a mature soul.

Resilience is the ability to envision new possibilities for what seems to be a hopeless or unmovable situation. This is digging deep and reminding yourself that you have the courage to take a breath and then another breath, that there is a way forward. You just have to craft it.

Humans can show great resilience even in the darkest hour of suffering and grief. We all know stories of people who survived the Holocaust, the genocide in Rwanda and Cambodia. These people have gone on to live meaningful lives, and they inspire us with their remarkable resilience. You don't have to endure great suffering to find your own resilience. Daily life can be tough and some days seem endless with crying children, constant interruptions, long to-do lists, difficult teenagers, stand-still traffic, demanding bosses, leaking roofs, broken cars, and ailing parents. On a pilgrimage, you may be faced with illness, physical pain, home-sickness, and anxiety. This is the place to remember that you have an inner strength to hold on until things improve. On a hard day, I just remind myself "this too shall pass."

Everyone has experienced failures, big and small, but we all have resilience inside us. Even when you think you can't, you can dust yourself off and accept the reality of the day you are living. Many times resilience looks like acceptance. Sometimes resilience means a change of attitude or perspective. It is these small changes that really make the pilgrimage to your heart, which is your real destination.

Day 27 - Confident You

As your pilgrim's path unfolds, your confidence is growing. As you reflect back on your life and look at the joys and sorrows, achievements and failures, you will see that you have—through it all—become unafraid of moving forward. This pilgrimage is a prayer to be more independent, relying on yourself for your own happiness and personal growth.

Achievement and resilience bring more confidence and self-reliance. You wouldn't have chosen to take a pilgrimage if you didn't have these traits. So, reflect on the times when you felt confident in your knowledge and skills these last few weeks. Everyone has areas of experience and expertise. What are yours? These skills don't have to be an intellectual or athletic. Your skills are how you navigate your world with confidence. Mothers know how to comfort their children. Some people know how to be present and expressive in tough situations. Others know how to run a business or cook a beautiful meal. Our contribution to the world doesn't need to be on the front page of the paper to be important. Everyone has their perfect part to play in the world.

When you bring your confidence to life then you have an independence of spirit that guides you. A pilgrimage builds confidence as you experience new places and people and as you negotiate an always changing environment. At the beginning of the Camino I was sometimes overwhelmed by the challenges of walking all day and then finding a place to eat and sleep at night. Everything was new, but as time went on, I gained confidence and wasn't so anxious. I was able to sink into the moment knowing I would be able to handle the next challenge. Not only did I grow mentally stronger but physically stronger too. One morning the first part of the trail was a very steep hill. I challenged myself to see if I could climb to the top without stopping. I went slowly, but I never had to stop to rest. I found confidence in my growing strength, and I enjoyed the challenge. When I got to the top of the hill and looked back down into the beautiful valley below, it was as if I had won a medal in my own personal Olympics. I was triumphant. It wasn't a big victory to the world, but this wasn't about the world. It was about me being a better, self-reliant person. I didn't need someone to help me or rely on someone else' opinion or approval. My own joy of accomplishment was all I needed.

When you stand in your joy and confidence, you raise the level of your life and all those around you. Your confidence will be contagious as you encourage those around to find their confidence in the little things that then led to bigger achievements and victories. It all starts with you climbing to the top of your hill, whatever that may be.

Day 28 - Conscious You

Today is the end of four full weeks on your quest. In the last 28 days, the moon has been full, has waned to dark and has waxed back to full. Just as our nearest cosmic neighbor has completed a cycle, so have you. You have dedicated yourself to spending a part of every day to examine your life in the past and your dreams for the future. But most importantly, I hope that you have focused your attention on the here and now, this very moment you are breathing. It is so easy for the mind to wander, but to be present and focused on the eternal now is how we grow.

How do we remain awake and aware so that every moment can be fully lived and felt? That is the question that seekers have been struggling with through the ages. Our minds seem to want to be everywhere else but right here, right now. Meditation and prayer are the time-tested techniques for a focused and peaceful mind. But how to achieve this in our fast-paced and ever-distracted world? It isn't always possible to sequester yourself and find periods of silence; this might not even be appealing to you. So what about staying aware and noticing?

Instead of closing yourself off from the world, become fully engaged in each moment. Become aware of your environment instead of just driving or walking through it mindlessly thinking about your next task. There is so much beauty all around us. Even in the cracks in the road, a plant finds a place to flourish. The sky above and the ground under your feet, the birds singing and the smell of the local bakery are all part of our daily world, treasures to be noticed and enjoyed rather than missed.

Part of your pilgrimage is stepping into the timelessness of our natural world and noticing the beauty and abundance that is everywhere. Use your whole consciousness to participate in your world: all five senses, your breath, and your intuition. Open your heart and mind to participate fully in all life has to offer. My wise teacher always says "We are in the glory now." The glory is all around us, but we only notice when we choose to stay aware.

Week 5

Actions

DAY 29 - WHAT DO YOU WANT?

As you begin your last full week of the pilgrimage, you may feel the need to set goals so that you can go home with a plan; a surety that you will have made this time useful. But I want to open you to the possibility that your usual methods of planning and achievement need to be shifted. You have changed, and the status quo must too.

So let's examine some new ideas on how to get your heart's desire. For me, the most wonderful experiences of my life were not written goals or on vision boards but subtle almost imperceptible moments when everything changed. Sometimes it was a book or an article in a newspaper, the words of a friend or just an idea in my mind. These tiny threads led me to experiences and joys that I could have never dreamed on my own. The realms of the Divine don't work by the same rules as our human business and culture. So, step out of the cultural model of bullet points and to-do lists, and choose instead to follow the call of the heart.

The way you know you are on the right path is by the synchronicities or meaningful coincidences that occur in your life. These can be in the form of an unexpected encounter in the grocery store; a book pushed out on the shelf, a link in a website or an overheard conversation that, for apparently no reason, turn out to be significant. These are life's guiding signposts. One thing subtly leads to the next. I took a very short pilgrimage based on an article I read in the Wall Street Journal about a garden in Alabama. That pilgrimage led to visit Helen Keller's childhood home nearby. On the way home I was listening to an interview that led me to the Joseph Campbell library in California a few weeks later. I had no idea at any point that a trip to California would open up a whole new direction for my life.

When you have dedicated to aligning with the Divine, you have to let your soul take over and lead you. Over the next few days, you will explore the desires of your heart that led you to this open-ended, joyful way of living life. The quality of each step and the love and effort you put into what is before you allows the next step to appear. By noticing your world and following your curiosity and passion, you become aware of possibilities that might not be part of the prescribed program of the world you have been living in. As you become open-hearted and expand your world, the Divine can find and use you in wonderful ways, ways you could never have imagined.

We don't work the mystery of life; we let the Mystery work us.

Day 30 - Focused You

As you examine your heart and mind for your true desires, you need to look at your values. In your values lay clues to your true path. What is important to you? Who is important to you? What do you need in order to bring congruency to your life? Sometimes you need to add something, but sometimes you need to get rid of the things that distract you. It is time to focus on your values.

What do you value in your life? We tend to get our priorities and values mixed-up and commandeered by the world. This pilgrimage is the time to get centered and sort out your top priorities, your true values. This is the time to take a step out of the mass mind and into your own individual mind, to choose what you want to focus on. Is it your personal growth, your family, engaging with the world, living the mystery, or contributing to humanity?

When you focus on these big questions, you clarify what you really hold dear. It is by coming into alignment with these core values that you live more authentically. An authentic life is one where you have deep respect and appreciation for your life, the lives around you and the world we all live in together.

At the Musee de Cluny—Musee National du Moyen Age in Paris are a series of magnificent tapestries -The Lady and the Unicorn. In all the six masterpiece tapestries are of an elegant lady enjoying the five senses until the final one "My Sole Desire" where she is standing with the mythical unicorn. She is leaving the call of worldly desires to follow her soul's desire symbolized by the elusive unicorn, a symbol of purity and grace. For it is this grace that brings fullness and joy to our lives. Our beautiful lady has chosen what she values when she chooses the unicorn. What is your unicorn?

Day 31 - Passionate You

When you first heard the call for your pilgrimage you probably felt very enthusiastic. Many times your destination is a place you have longed for, a place that calls you and holds a piece of yourself that you are looking for. You may have read or watched things about your holy spot. Your passion for finding and living your best life has brought you to this place. Even if your call was motivated by repairing what was broken in your life, at the heart of it is the desire to live your fullest life.

A world without passion is gray and flat, colorless and lifeless. It is passion that gives us the eagerness to live. What fascinated you as a child? Usually, you can reflect back on a subject or skill that you spent hours studying or pursuing. Where is that passion today, is it still part of your everyday life. Our childhood passions come from the purity of our soul, not from the dictates of the world, and therefore are a key to our deep longing. Childhood passions lead us to a place where we can reconnect with ourselves.

I always had a love of music and reading, they were an integral part of my family life, and I spent my childhood playing the piano and reading classic children's literature, such as Anne of Green Gables, Little House on the Prairie, Heidi and Little Women. These strong girls were my role models, and their stories gave me a passion for freedom and independence that I have never outgrown. My passion for music led me to start my daughters on violin at a very young age, and we spent their childhood making music together and traveling for performances. My passion became their passion too.

Maybe you have new passions that you discovered as an adult. If you have outgrown these or have allowed them to fall by the wayside, it is time to bring these joys back into your days. Passion is where we find our creativity in its many forms and is about bringing beauty and joy into life. Passion is the mother of enthusiasm, a word that comes from the Greek entheos—inspired by God. The Divine spark lives in your passions and joys.

Day 32 - Intentional You

People talk a lot about setting an intention. But what does this really mean? Just because you think good thoughts and want something to work out, it will? We all know that isn't true. We all know people who talk a good game, but nothing will come of their 'plans.' Intention isn't about meaning to do something or merely positive thinking. Intention is a thought that becomes action toward your goal. You can talk about making a pilgrimag, but without taking specific steps to make plans and set aside the time, it will add to the pile of unfulfilled dreams that weigh on your soul.

Intentional can also mean purposeful and deliberate, this is where the secret to manifestation lies. As you move through this week of examining your values and passions, you need to add this purposefulness of action. If you don't make the steps, then inertia will take over, and you won't like the outcome, and your life remains stagnant. There is a level of practicality that comes with intention. You might not know every step you will take, but you must at least know the direction and take the first step. With each step, you leave behind inertia and move into momentum. Then the next step will always follow naturally. Do you need to make a phone call or read a particular book, make a reservation or sell something? With each purposeful movement, your intentions become manifest.

Intentional also can mean thoughtful and meaningful. Not only do you take deliberate steps, but you assign a greater meaning to your action. As you spend time at the place you have longed for, you become purposeful in your thoughts and actions. The respect you give these holy places brings that respect back to you. You learn to respect yourself, and the world around you, just as you are. I often like to take a traditional offering of sage or holy oil to a sacred site. It is this act of honor and respect that makes the moment intentional—movement and desire coming together. I may not know the traditional words or understand the complete history of the site, but I make a moment of deliberate intention, giving the experience a fullness that I know demonstrates my devotion to the Divine and my life here on this earth.

Day 33 - Inspired You

Dreams, passions, deliberate actions—all the things you've been cultivating this week—lead to creativity. All of these things are part of the essence of inspiration, the vital breath of our creative being. Taking a pilgrimage comes from a moment of inspiration. The Call to a quest comes from a moment when our spirit calls us to something larger. In these moments where you have the spark of a new idea, a goal then brings a new dimension to your life.

A pilgrimage will not solve all your problems, but it will

give you the space to let the light of inspiration into your heart and mind. In history, true inspiration was considered a moment of Divine influence. It is hard to hear some of the great music of Mozart and Bach or see the luminous angel painting of Fra Angelico without seeing the Divine revealed. We see and hear the moments of great revelation all around us in beautiful architecture, original music, great art and deeply humanitarian acts. The Divine is always with us in our every moment, whether we acknowledge it or not.

Inspiration and the influence of Divine creativity can become part of your everyday world. It is about being in the moment, present with what your day brings. Finding a creative moment of play with your child, a walk with the birds and trees, a kind word to a stranger, a sweet note to your grandmother, a refusal to participate in negative talk—all these acts can lead to these special moments.

I like to start my day with a hot cup of coffee, my cat Timmy on my lap and a book of spiritual inspiration. For just a few simple, quiet moments in the early morning, I commune with other minds and hearts of people who touched the Divine. It is important to take a bit of time morning or evening, or both, to meditate, read or pray – anything you choose as a ritual to center yourself in the still point where inspiration can find you. I know during a particularly trying time in my life, it was only after an hour of yoga and the quiet rest at the end that I was able to relax my mind and body enough to find peace, to tap into my higher self and find the inspiration I needed to make the right choices.

Your pilgrimage contains these moments of inspiration, great or small, that will open the next door, or maybe even a small window, that lets the Divine light of awakening into your life. You have asked for these insights and moments of deep peace. They are there for you when you are ready.

Day 34 - Faithful You

The next step in making the life you want is faithfully acting on your inspiration and fulfilling your intentions. Nothing will happen if you don't honor your word and do what you said you would do. You have made a promise to yourself to change things. Broken promises lead to so much heartache, hurt feelings, unfinished business, lost opportunities and ruined relationships. Over the last five weeks, you have strengthened and examined your inner self so that you can be more faithful to yourself and those you love.

Consistency and reliability are some of the most important skills and characteristics a pilgrim can have. So much of the world is unreliable that just the ability to show up and do what you said you would do is often the most important part of your work. It doesn't matter if you have great talent or brilliant ideas unless you can put them into action. Make good on your promises, follow through on your word and honor your vows.

Your pilgrimage brings you closer to the luminous world of the Divine. When you bring that elusive quality of faith into your life and heart, then divinity is more available to you. In our physical world, we want to prove everything and make sure that our ideas and beliefs are tangible. This mechanical quality has its place in everyday life but often fails in matters of the heart and our spiritual life. We all have had unprovable and irrational experiences. There is always a component of faith in the inexplicable moments of life.

Your pilgrimage is an act of faith, believing with all

your heart that what you seek, you will find. When you work steadfastly toward a goal, you must always have faith that your effort will bring the desired outcome. You must have faith in yourself and in the Divine. The outcomes you desire and work for may not be what's best for you. When you have taken the actions for your goal but are blocked at every turn, then the Divine has something better in mind for you. It can be hard and unnerving when our hopes and dreams don't work out, but the best things in my life were the unplanned opportunities. So many times I didn't even know to dream a certain dream, but with a receptive state teacher, travel, friendships and experiences have shown up beyond my imagination.

Day 35 - Grateful You

As your forty days are drawing to a close, it is time to reflect on your experiences and new insights. Take a look at your story and see how your life has led you to this moment. By taking these weeks out of your everyday life and giving yourself the beautiful gift of time, you have opened yourself to the great creativity and abundance of our Divine world. I'm sure you have had moments of sorrow and also amazing moments of gratitude.

Along with your journey, you have experience kindness from others, and I'm sure ' returned kindness too. This give-and-take in life is part of the wonderful web of open-spiritedness that characterizes the journey of the pilgrim. You have laid yourself bare to the quest and opened your heart and mind to the joys and challenges of a larger world. You have gained a new perspective on your life and the beautiful earth where we live. I hope that every day has contained moments of deep gratitude for the privilege of your life and this journey. For despite the highs and lows of life, we are so privileged to have a life and the opportunity to travel and learn.

From gratitude comes joy and delight, the very essence of a spirit-filled life. This appreciation allows you to treasure your life and all life. When you acknowledge the beauty of life, you see it in others. The beautiful word Namaste, repeated at the end of yoga classes, reminds us "The divine in me bows to the divine in you." I can't think of a more fitting way to show appreciation.

I occasionally come across someone that seems to lack gratitude and appreciation; this usually comes with a great deal of self-centeredness. There is a quality of entitlement to their life, and I have yet to find these people happy. I'm sure you have experienced such people. They are very tiring and difficult. Nothing you do for them is enough or makes them happy. In contrast, when you are around people that are respectful and grateful, you feel energized and delighted.

In the last few years, gratitude diaries have become popular, and that is a beautiful thing. By taking a few minutes, morning or evening, to reflect on the delightful moments, treasured friends and family, physical comfort and beauty give another moment for your heart to enter that luminous state where the Divine resides. When I stand in some of the most sacred places on earth, I'm filled with gratitude for the privilege of being there. On my trip to Southeast Asia, I went to see the great Buddhist temples with the gold Buddha. I lacked the traditional words and rituals, but my gratitude for the enlightened path of the Buddha was all that I needed. When words fail, a grateful heart steps in to bring your pilgrim moment to perfection.

Week 6

Destiny

Day 36 - How Can I Serve?

As you come to the last few days of your pilgrimage, you start to think about your reentry into everyday life. When you first started your journey, 40 days seemed a long time and far away. But somehow time passes, and you must return home. In these final few days concentrate on celebrating your journey and preparing for your return and integration back into life. You need to take care of your family and pets, return to work and all the demands of taking care of a home. Ultimately, it isn't a pilgrimage without a return.

In the myths of heroic journeys, the pilgrim/hero comes back with information or material to inform the village or society. You too have to bring home what you have learned and inform your world. This isn't about making everyone hear the details or see the pictures of your adventures. I've actually found that all I usually tell people is the basic facts of pilgrimage, and maybe show them a few pictures of the sacred site. They don't really want to hear about my inner transformation. Quite frankly, most people can't imagine this type of interior journey and wouldn't understand the experience. I recommend not oversharing the details of your trip or your insights. These are your private joys, and you need not disperse the energy or open yourself to criticism. Integration of your experience takes time, so give yourself time to let it all sink in. You need time to reflect and let the new wisdom infuse and inform your world.

You might be coming back with new plans and decisions for your life but most of all you return strengthened and empowered with self-knowledge and experiences. You bring back these qualities to improve your life and those around you. You may have great inspiration to serve humanity on a large scale or maybe to bring joy and peace to your corner of the world. All is service.

As you journey these last few days, allow yourself to enjoy the final moments of your quest. Sometimes it isn't about having everything figured out or all your questions answered but about being fully awake to your life as it is right now. When you dedicate yourself to becoming your true self, it takes awhile for the changes to filter into your everyday world. So be patient with yourself and don't worry if you don't have a clear plan. Your dedication and the changes you have made will bring about the next steps for your life.

A few weeks after my walk on the Camino I was asked to make a presentation to a small church group about my pilgrimage, and that led to other contacts and new friends and a new way to volunteer in my community. It is a small act of service, but these openings continue to be important in my growth and to bless others. I have also met and encouraged others who wanted to walk the Camino. I know that their lives were changed by the experience, too. And so it goes.

Day 37 - Unique You

One of the wonderful things about our world is the great varieties of life with infinite expressions. With the limitless possibilities of DNA that create each human, there is never a duplicate. Then you add the many cultures, climates, religions, governments, and families of each person, as well as their own psychological makeup. All of this boggles the mind when you think about the 7.5 billion people on the planet, right now, much less for the history of humanity. All of us have come to learn and grow within our unique life expression, and in our current world, we have even more possibilities with technology and travel to explore our world far from the bounds of our places of origin.

On your quest, you have reflected on the parts of your life that are unique to you and not anyone else. Your pilgrimage has been unlike anyone's before you. Even if you were on a journey with many others, your moment at your destination was yours alone. In the midst of humanity, you still stand on your own ground and feel your own emotions. Your wonderful, unique self is your gift to the world.

This new clarity about your life brings the opportunities to share your unique voice. Your perspective and experience are what is needed and why you went on the quest.

What stories do you have to tell to encourage others? What compassion can you give people who are experiencing similar trials? How can you help others find their own inner strength by experiencing yours? I know my tales from faraway lands have influenced others to travel and stand in their power. I encourage my friends and family to see the places that call them and go experience a larger world. Hopefully, my love of walking has inspired others to take a daily walk and go on an adventure. You may never know what you have inspired others to try, but that is OK. It is not necessary to know how our gifts to the world are being used—that is up to the Divine. Your job is to share your gifts just by being your authentic, unique you.

Day 38 - Extraordinary You

To ask for more for your life and taking action to find it is extraordinary. So many people want more but fear an extraordinary life. Ordinary is comfortable. Ordinary is safe. People don't want you to step into your power because it reminds them that they are stuck and unhappy. But your personal power is part of the new you and the way that you can make your life unique and meaningful. For a truly fulfilled life doesn't mean you have to be famous or wealthy. A fulfilled life has personal meaning and is grounded in service to the Divine.

Over the last few weeks, you have stripped away some of the old definitions of your life. It is going to take time to learn to live without some of these crutches, and you will have people unsettled by some of the changes in your life. Give yourself and others time to make the shift. You have moved, and others are unconsciously responding to the new you. Be patient with yourself and others, give yourself plenty of time and space. As you take more journeys of self-discovery, you will get used to the shifts that come with each new journey and insight.

As you find your remarkable personal power, you open your life to live out the genius that is particular to your life. This isn't about winning a Nobel prize but about the special way you interact with the world and the gifts you have to bring to the world both physically and spiritually. Remember that you must come to your life daily ready to use these new gifts. Like a musician who has to practice daily to keep their divinely given talent, you too have to make your life a daily act of devotion to the mystery and miracles that make the extraordinary moments of life. Every day is an extraordinary gift to be lived fully.

Day 39 - Visionary You

Our world celebrates visionaries, people who bring new technology, political and humanitarian solutions and scientific discoveries to the world. You, too, are a visionary, for you heard the Call, met the challenge, lived the mystery and returned to inform your life with wisdom and experience. You might not think that you have done something so extraordinary, but you have.

You have climbed to the metaphorical mountaintop of your life and looked out onto the vast horizon of your future. You might not be able to see individual trees and lakes but you now have a new view, a new perspective. The details will fill in as you move forward with this beautiful new perspective. When you have opened more deeply to the Divine in your life, you learn that you have this connection and live in alignment with the Universe and then you have the ability to co-create your life.

If you are just living unconsciously with no connection to

your deeper self, then you are subject to the whims and desires of the world. Stepping out into a more soulful life brings new attitudes and opportunities to explore new mountains, valleys, oceans, and lakes. By taking this heroic quest, you are the hero of your own life. There will always be new challenges to face, but you now have the strength and skills to handle what life brings. It isn't about having a perfect map and plan. It's about walking through life with grace and joy. It's about seeing the places you can apply your gifts and talents. Most of all, it's about finding where you can bring love and compassion to life.

The last few days of my Camino journey were spent at the final destination, Santiago in northwestern Spain. This beautiful city has been the great desire of pilgrims for a millennium. I arrived on Pentecost, the day Jesus' disciples received the Holy Spirit and were sent into the world to teach. This day symbolized the end of my learning stage and the beginning of bringing my new vision to the world. I was glad I had several days in that beautiful cathedral to rest and soak in the experience that I had shared with millions of pilgrims throughout history. I participated in the traditional pilgrim rituals, sang the songs, said the prayers and watched the great Botafumeiro fly through the cathedral blessing all of us. All of these acts reinforced my vision and gave me a grand finale to my quest. I was ready to return and start the new phase of my life.

There is a saying on the Camino – the real Camino begins when you return home—for your pilgrimage will always be with you informing the rest of your life, supporting you as you live out your vision.

Day 40 - Abundant World

On this final day, I'm sure you will look back on your journey with a bit of nostalgia. You will have time to remember the hard and challenging times but also the joyful and beautiful experience. It is hard to believe that this wonderful expansive experience is over. You might not be ready to reenter the world but are anxious to see those you love. No matter what, you are returning with an overflowing heart and mind that bring true spiritual abundance to your life.

When you have this spiritual, joyful abundance, then the world takes on a new beauty and glow. You no longer see abundance from the world's traditional definition of material wealth but from the Divine realms of beauty and peace. This world has so much to offer, and the overflowing expressions of the natural world are there when you have the eyes to see.

As unique and extraordinary as you are, ultimately the joy of living is in harmony with those around you. We all have to share our one wonderful planet. When you have found your joy and compassion, then you find the same in your fellow humans. By starting with your corner of the world, peace can move out from there and join with those who have the same desire. As you have quested, journeyed, walked, and discovered, you join with all the pilgrims through history who had the same goal: to seek the Divine with the humble heart of devotion and to enter the mystery of life.

Conclusion

The great mystic poet, Rumi wrote,

"40 early mornings does for the soul
what nine months of gestation does for the unborn child."

If 40 mornings nurture the soul, just imagine what 40 days of devotion to your inner world have done to inform the rest of your life. As you have spent your remarkable journey in the world expanding your knowledge and experience, your inner world has become equally re-enchanted with the magic of living your unique life.

The challenges and joys of a pilgrimage interconnect with the challenges and joys of your interior life and together give an entirely new mission for your life. This may be subtle or dramatic or somewhere in between, but rest assured that your life going forward will be different. As you grow, new questions and tests will come up, and the Call to another place in the world will bring you deeper into your life. This is the never-ending cycle of being human.

You've taken time out of your everyday life to find a special time to live life to its fullest, started new conversations with your most authentic self, and found the courage and resilience to face this complex world. But mostly, I hope that you have found joy. For it is in joy that we feel and experience the Divine world. It is the moments of pure joy that align us with this benevolent and beautiful world we live in. It is this two-fold relationship with the joy of the world and the joy of your life that bring you to this rebirth, this re-imagining of your world.

You are connected with pilgrims throughout history and now into the future. The year I walked the Camino was the 800th anniversary of St. Francis of Assisi's Camino journey. I went to the Franciscan monastery next to the Santiago cathedral where I presented my pilgrim log full of stamps from the hostels and churches. Each stamp was a mark in the book and also a new experience for my life. The monk carefully wrote my name on the certificate commemorating this important anniversary. I walked in the footsteps of the saint.

Thomas Merton wrote, "For me to be a saint is to be myself." You are part of the longing of the human soul to be devoted to the Divinity made visible in the world, and therefore the Divinity in yourself. By stepping on the infinite pilgrim path, you have become a saint just by being your remarkable self.

I wish you well on your extraordinary journey of the pilgrim's path.

Favorite Pilgrimage Sites

My Favorite International Sacred Sites:

+Egypt— Pyramids and Sphynx, Luxor Temples.
+Jordan— Petra
+England— Stonehenge, Glastonbury, Canterbury Cathedral
+France— Chartres Cathedral, Unicorn Tapestries— Museum de Moyen Age
+Spain— Santiago and Burgos Cathedrals, Alhambra
+Scotland— Rosslyn Chapel, Callanish Standing Stones
+Peru—Machu Picchu, Saksaywaman
+Cambodia—Angkor Wat
+Thailand—Wat Traimit

My Favorite American Sacred Sites:

+Great Serpent Mound, Ohio
+Great Tetons and Yellowstone, Wyoming
+Looking Glass Rock, North Carolina
+Ave Maria Grotto, Alabama
+Mesa Verde, Colorado
+Huntington Gardens and Library, California
+Grand Canyon, Arizona
+Cleopatra's Needle, Central Park, New York
+Chaco Canyon, New Mexico
+Muir Woods, California

About the Author

Evans Bowen is the creator of The Perpetual Pilgrim, a travel blog inspired by her life of sacred travel. Always a traveler, Evans has been to all 50 states, Peru, Egypt, Jordan, Europe, Thailand, Taiwan, and Cambodia. In 2014 she walked the 500 miles of the Camino to Santiago, Spain with her 20 year old daughter, Alexandra. This 40 day pilgrimage inspired this book. Evans has a BA in Education from the University of Tennessee and is currently working on an MA in Depth Psychology from Pacifica Graduate Institute. When not visiting sacred sites, she lives a quiet life in an old farmhouse in rural east Tennessee with her husband, two cats, and lots of books.

Acknowledgments

I first want to thank my dear friend and spiritual sister Val for gifting me a tiny pack of handwritten cards just days before my Camino pilgrimage. These small cards gave me great courage along the way and the inspiration for this book. You sent me off with cards and met me at the end with clothes. I'd like to thank my dear friend and mentor the late Page Bryant, she told me I would some day write a book and encouraged my every step. A master of earth energies, sacred sites and ceremony, I learned from the best. To my spiritual mother and teacher Rachael Salley. You taught me to live in the moment and allow life to flow. You showed me how to capture intuition and apply it to everyday life.

I want to thank my fellow pilgrims on the journey; Darrell, Glen, Mary, Judy, Melynie, Jenny, Miriam, and Joanne, and so many other dear friends that shared the joy along the way. A special thanks to my daughter Alexandra who insisted we walk in Spain and is now trekking around the globe.

Thanks goes to my daughter Caroline who has taken me on the journey to the infinite world of the universe, the invisible world of quantum and the enigma of mathematics.

Thanks to my father Millard who taught me to love a daily walk, the true fountain of youth. Thanks to my mother Sue for her loving support of my many travels.

Most of all to my husband Hamilton who kept the home fires burning while I yet again headed out to my next adventure. You have supported my every step and are an amazing companion on the journey of life.

CPSIA information can be obtained
at www.ICGtesting.com
Printed in the USA
BVHW04s2126300718
522769BV00011B/217/P

9 781936 426409